Netscape 2

—S I M P L I F I E D—

VISUAL 3D SERIES

by: maranGraphics' Development Group

Corporate Sales

Contact maranGraphics
Phone: (905) 890-3300
(800) 469-6616
Fax: (905) 890-9434

Canadian Trade Sales

Contact Prentice Hall Canada
Phone: (416) 293-3621
(800) 567-3800
Fax: (416) 299-2529

Visit our Web site at:
http://www.maran.com

Netscape 2 Simplified

Copyright©   1995, 1996 by maranGraphics Inc.
5755 Coopers Avenue
Mississauga, Ontario, Canada
L4Z 1R9

Canadian Cataloguing in Publication Data

Maran, Ruth, 1970-
    Netscape 2 simplified

(Visual 3-D series)
Written by Ruth Maran.
Includes index.
ISBN 1-896283-19-5

1. Netscape. 2. World Wide Web (Information retrieval
system) . 3. Internet (Computer network).
I. maranGraphics' Development Group. II. MaranGraphics Inc.
III. Title. IV. Series.

TK5105.882.M37 1996   025.04   C96-930641-5

Trademark Acknowledgments

maranGraphics Inc. has attempted to include trademark information for products, services and companies referred to in this guide. Although maranGraphics Inc. has made reasonable efforts in gathering this information, it cannot guarantee its accuracy.

All other brand names and product names used in this book are trademarks, registered trademarks, or trade names of their respective holders. maranGraphics Inc. is not associated with any product or vendor mentioned in this book.

Screen Shot Acknowledgments

*Every maranGraphics book represents
the extraordinary vision and commitment of a unique family:
the Maran family of Toronto, Canada.*

Back Row (from left to right): *Sherry Maran, Rob Maran, Richard Maran, Maxine Maran, Jill Maran.*
Front Row (from left to right): *Judy Maran, Ruth Maran.*

Richard Maran is the company founder and its inspirational leader. He developed maranGraphics' proprietary communication technology called "visual grammar." This book is built on that technology—empowering readers with the easiest and quickest way to learn about computers.

Ruth Maran is the Author and Architect—a role Richard established that now bears Ruth's distinctive touch. She creates the words and visual structure that are the basis for the books.

Judy Maran is Senior Editor. She works with Ruth, Richard, and the highly talented maranGraphics illustrators, designers, and editors to transform Ruth's material into its final form.

Rob Maran is the Technical and Production Specialist. He makes sure the state-of-the-art technology used to create these books always performs as it should.

Sherry Maran manages the Reception, Order Desk, and any number of areas that require immediate attention and a helping hand.

Jill Maran is a jack-of-all-trades and dynamo who fills in anywhere she's needed anytime she's back from university.

Maxine Maran is the Business Manager and family sage. She maintains order in the business and family—and keeps everything running smoothly.

Oh, and three other family members are seated on the sofa. These graphic disk characters help make it fun and easy to learn about computers. They're part of the extended maranGraphics family.

Credits

Author & Architect:
Ruth Maran

Copy Developer & Editor:
Kelleigh Wing

Technical Consultant:
Neil Mohan

Project Manager:
Judy Maran

Editors:
Alison MacAlpine
Susan Beytas

Proofreader:
Brad Hilderley

Layout Designers:
Christie Van Duin
Tamara Poliquin

Illustrators:
Chris K.C. Leung
Russell Marini
Andrew Trowbridge
Greg Midensky

Screen Artist:
Julie Lane

Indexer:
Kelleigh Wing

Post Production:
Robert Maran

Acknowledgments

Thanks to the dedicated staff of maranGraphics, including Susan Beytas, Francisco Ferreira, Brad Hilderley, Julie Lane, Chris K.C. Leung, Alison MacAlpine, Jill Maran, Judy Maran, Maxine Maran, Robert Maran, Sherry Maran, Russ Marini, Greg Midensky, Tamara Poliquin, Andrew Trowbridge, Christie Van Duin and Kelleigh Wing.

Finally, to Richard Maran who originated the easy-to-use graphic format of this guide. Thank you for your inspiration and guidance.

TABLE OF CONTENTS

CHAPTER 1

INTRODUCTION

CHAPTER 2

NAVIGATE THE WEB

CHAPTER 3

STORE WEB PAGES

— CHAPTER

TIME-SAVING FEATURES

— CHAPTER

SEARCH THE WEB

— CHAPTER

MULTIMEDIA ON THE WEB

TABLE OF CONTENTS

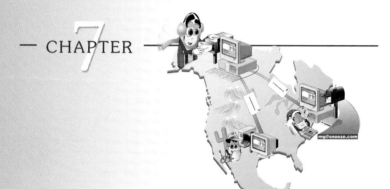

NEWSGROUP BASICS

WORK WITH ARTICLES

80 COOL WEB SITES

INTRODUCTION

 Introduction to the Internet

 How Information Transfers

 Introduction to the Web

 Introduction to Netscape

INTRODUCTION TO THE INTERNET

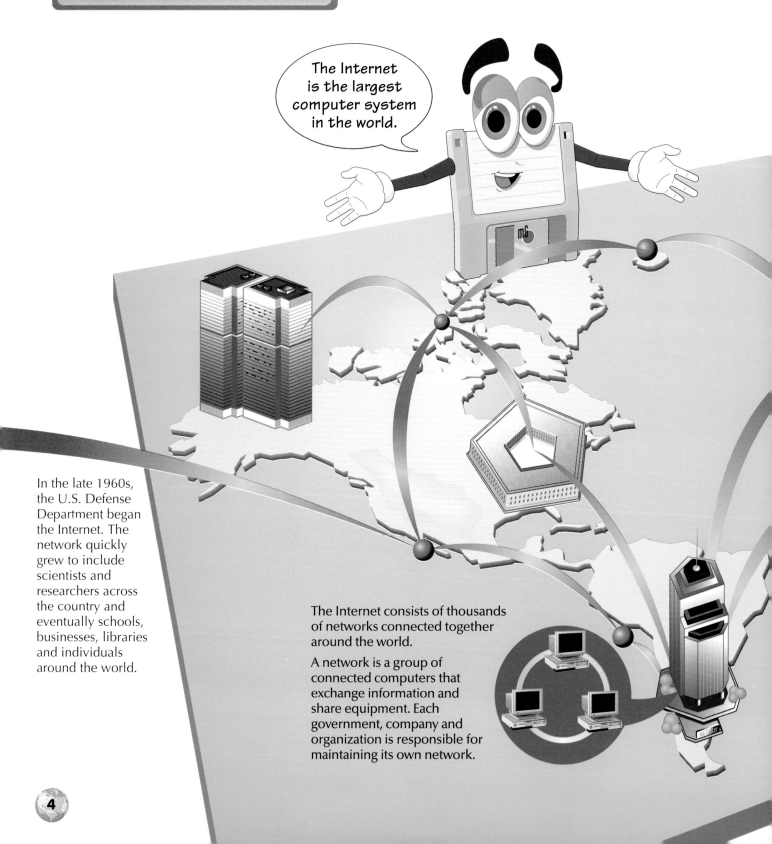

The Internet is the largest computer system in the world.

In the late 1960s, the U.S. Defense Department began the Internet. The network quickly grew to include scientists and researchers across the country and eventually schools, businesses, libraries and individuals around the world.

The Internet consists of thousands of networks connected together around the world.

A network is a group of connected computers that exchange information and share equipment. Each government, company and organization is responsible for maintaining its own network.

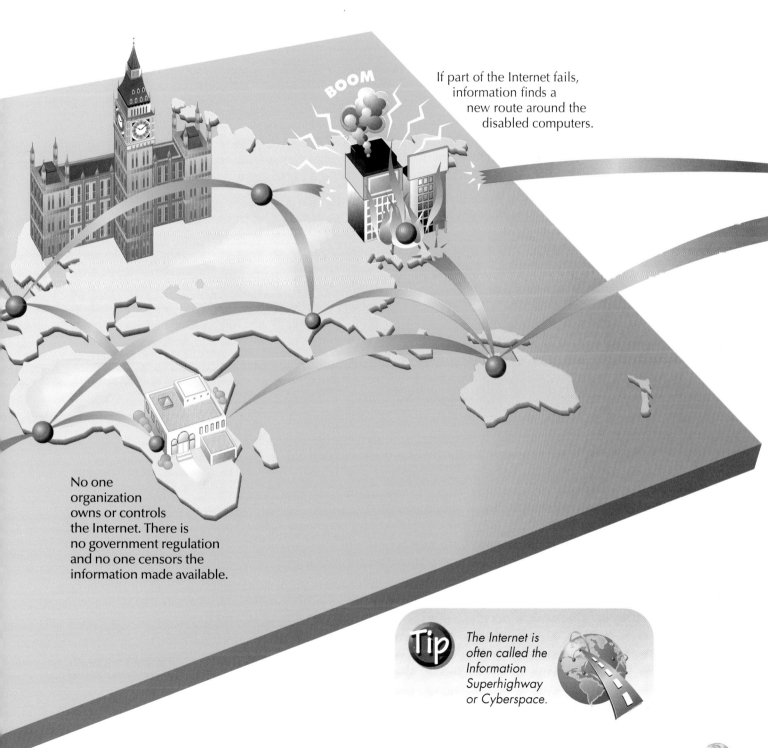

If part of the Internet fails, information finds a new route around the disabled computers.

No one organization owns or controls the Internet. There is no government regulation and no one censors the information made available.

Tip The Internet is often called the Information Superhighway or Cyberspace.

All computers on the Internet work together to transfer information back and forth around the world.

Modem

A modem exchanges information between your computer and the Internet. You should have a modem with a speed of at least 14,400 bps, but a 28,800 bps modem is recommended.

Service Provider

A service provider is a company that gives you access to the Internet for a fee.

Who Pays for the Internet?

There are no long distance charges for sending or receiving information on the Internet. Once you pay for your connection to the Internet, you can exchange information free of charge.

Companies, government agencies, colleges and universities around the world pay to operate and maintain their part of the Internet. When you send information, organizations along the way pay for the information that passes through their networks. This lets you avoid long distance charges.

Router

Routers are specialized computers that regulate the traffic on the Internet. A packet may pass through many routers before reaching its intended destination.

Like a good travel agent, a router picks the most efficient route, based on the traffic and the number of stopovers.

T1 and T3

T1 and T3 are high-speed computer lines that carry information between huge computer systems on the Internet.

Packet

When you send information through the Internet, the information is broken down into smaller pieces, called packets. Each packet travels independently through the Internet and may take a different path to arrive at the intended destination.

When information arrives at the intended destination, the packets are reassembled. If a packet arrives damaged, the computer that sent the packet is asked to send a new copy.

INTRODUCTION TO THE WEB

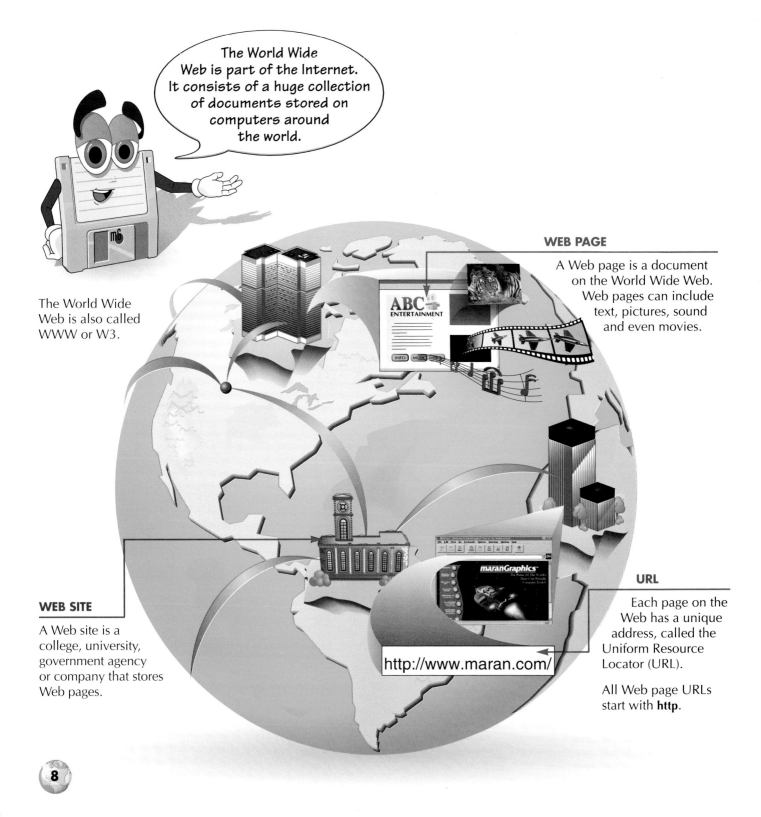

The World Wide Web is part of the Internet. It consists of a huge collection of documents stored on computers around the world.

The World Wide Web is also called WWW or W3.

WEB PAGE

A Web page is a document on the World Wide Web. Web pages can include text, pictures, sound and even movies.

ABC ENTERTAINMENT

INFO   MUSIC

maranGraphics

http://www.maran.com/

WEB SITE

A Web site is a college, university, government agency or company that stores Web pages.

URL

Each page on the Web has a unique address, called the Uniform Resource Locator (URL).

All Web page URLs start with **http**.

WEB PAGES ARE CONNECTED

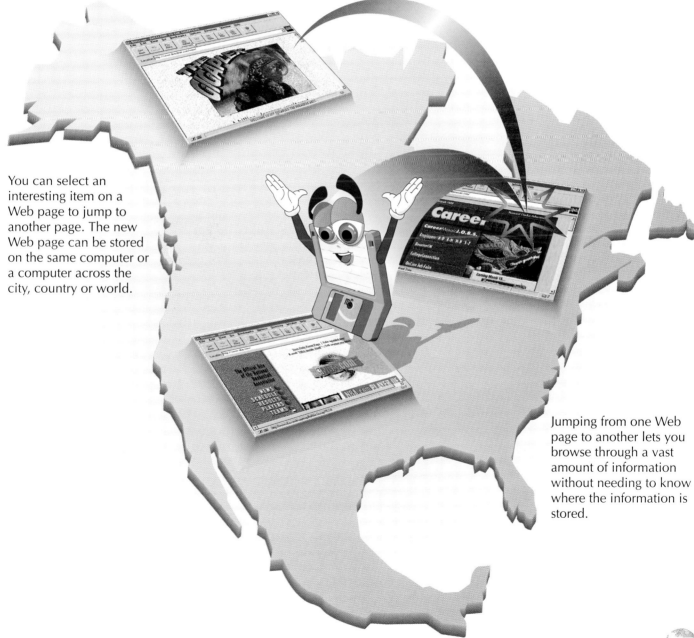

You can select an interesting item on a Web page to jump to another page. The new Web page can be stored on the same computer or a computer across the city, country or world.

Jumping from one Web page to another lets you browse through a vast amount of information without needing to know where the information is stored.

Netscape Navigator™ 2 is a program that lets you view and explore information on the World Wide Web.

GET INFORMATION

Netscape lets you browse through information on the Web. You can find information on any subject imaginable. You can review newspapers, magazines, academic papers, government documents, television show transcripts, famous speeches, recipes, job listings, works by Shakespeare, airline schedules and much more.

You can also buy items such as flowers, used cars, computer programs, music CDs and pizza without ever leaving your desk.

EXCHANGE ELECTRONIC MAIL

Netscape lets you exchange electronic mail with people around the world. This can include friends, colleagues, family members, customers and even people you meet on the Internet. Electronic mail is fast, easy, inexpensive and saves paper.

JOIN NEWSGROUPS

Netscape lets you join discussion groups, called newsgroups, to meet people around the world with similar interests. You can ask questions, discuss problems and read interesting stories. There are thousands of discussion groups on topics such as the environment, food, humor, music, pets, photography, politics, religion, sports and television.

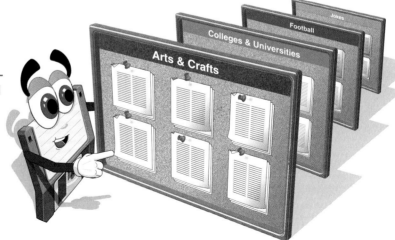

CHAPTER

NAVIGATE THE WEB

 Start and Exit Netscape

 Change the Screen Display

 Display a Specific Web Page

 Select a Link

 Stop Loading a Page

 Scroll Through a Page

 Move Through Pages

 Using Frames

 Connect to a Secure Site

 Reload a Page

 Change Toolbar Appearance

 Using the Directory Buttons

 Error Messages

START AND EXIT NETSCAPE

Netscape is a program that lets you view and explore information on the Web.

START NETSCAPE

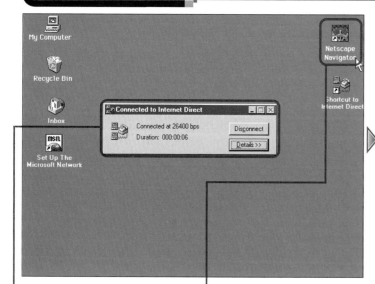

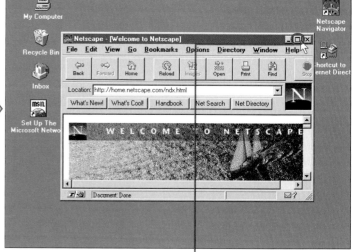

1 Before starting Netscape, connect to your service provider using a program such as Trumpet Winsock or the Microsoft Dial-Up Networking feature.

*Note: In this example, we are using the Microsoft Dial-Up Networking feature. For more information, refer to the **Tip** on page 15.*

2 Move the mouse ⟍ over **Netscape Navigator** and then quickly press the left button twice.

■ The Netscape window appears, displaying your home page. Your home page appears every time you start the program.

Note: To change your home page, refer to page 64.

3 To enlarge the Netscape window to fill your screen, move the mouse ⟍ over ▢ and then press the left button.

Tip

You need two programs to browse through information on the Web.

You need a program to manage the transfer of information between your computer and the Web.

Popular programs include Trumpet Winsock and the Microsoft Dial-Up Networking feature.

You need a program to view and explore information on the Web. Netscape is currently the most popular program.

EXIT NETSCAPE

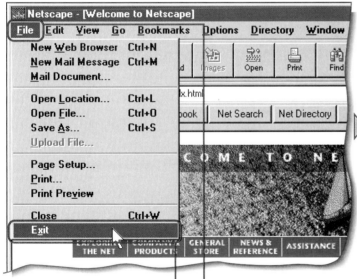

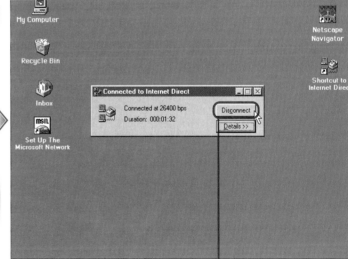

When you finish exploring information on the Web, exit Netscape.

1 Move the mouse over **File** and then press the left button.

2 Move the mouse over **Exit** and then press the left button.

■ The Netscape window disappears from your screen.

3 Disconnect from your service provider.

CHANGE THE SCREEN DISPLAY

Netscape provides three bars to help you browse through information on the Web. You can easily hide or display these bars at any time.

CHANGE THE SCREEN DISPLAY

Toolbar

Displays buttons that provide shortcuts for common tasks.

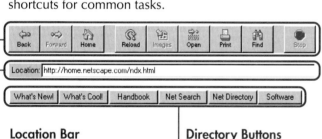

Location Bar

Displays the address of the page you are viewing.

Directory Buttons

Displays buttons that let you quickly access interesting and useful information on the Web.

1 To change the screen display, move the mouse over **Options** and then press the left button.

■ Items displaying a check mark (✔) are currently displayed on your screen.

2 To hide an item, move the mouse over the item and then press the left button.

Tip

The Toolbar, Location bar and Directory Buttons take up space on your screen. If you do not use one or more of these bars, you can remove them to provide a larger viewing area.

With Bars   Without Bars

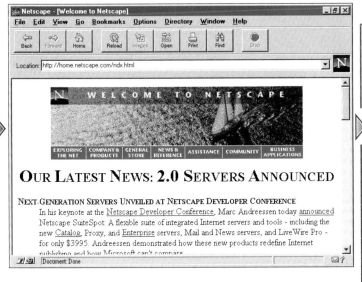

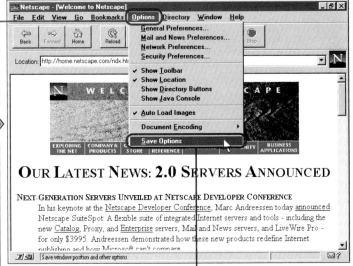

■ The item disappears.

■ To redisplay an item you have hidden, repeat steps **1** and **2**.

3 If you want Netscape to remember the changes you made the next time you start the program, move the mouse ⬍ over **Options** and then press the left button.

4 Move the mouse ⬍ over **Save Options** and then press the left button.

DISPLAY A SPECIFIC WEB PAGE

You can easily display a page on the Web that you have heard or read about.

http://www.maran.com

To display a specific Web page, you need to know the address of the page, called the URL. Each page on the Web has a unique URL.

DISPLAY A SPECIFIC WEB PAGE

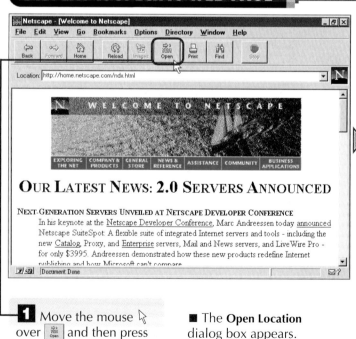

1 Move the mouse ⬚ over [Open] and then press the left button.

■ The **Open Location** dialog box appears.

2 Type the address of the Web page you want to view.

Note: Addresses are case-sensitive. Make sure you enter upper and lower case letters exactly.

3 Move the mouse ⬚ over **Open** and then press the left button.

Tip

Netscape remembers the last addresses you typed in the Location bar, even when you turn off your computer. You can select one of these addresses to quickly return to a Web page.

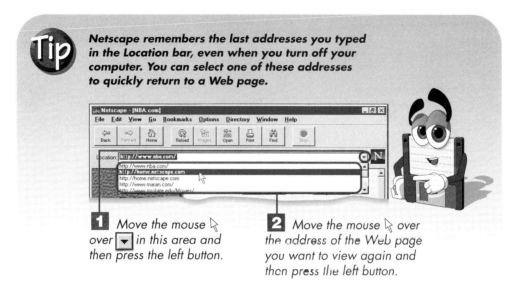

1 Move the mouse ⟍ over ▾ in this area and then press the left button.

2 Move the mouse ⟍ over the address of the Web page you want to view again and then press the left button.

■ The Web page appears on your screen.

Note: Companies frequently change their Web pages to make the pages more attractive or to add additional information. Therefore, the Web pages you see in this book may look different from the Web pages displayed on your screen.

You can also display a specific Web page by typing the address in the Location bar.

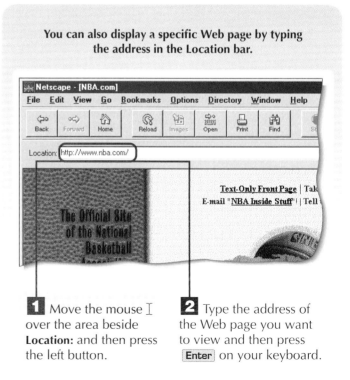

1 Move the mouse I over the area beside **Location:** and then press the left button.

2 Type the address of the Web page you want to view and then press Enter on your keyboard.

SELECT A LINK

> Pages on the Web are connected. This lets you easily move between pages stored in the same city, across the country or around the world.

SELECT A LINK

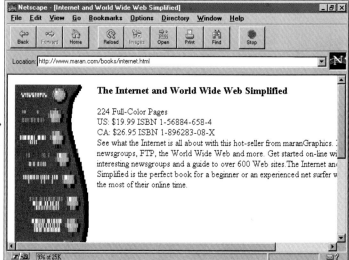

■ Highlighted words and many pictures are linked to other pages on the Web.

1 Move the mouse ▷ over a highlighted word or picture of interest.

■ If the mouse ▷ changes to 🖑, you can select the word or picture to display the page connected to the item.

2 To select the word or picture, press the left button.

■ Netscape displays the page connected to the word or picture you selected.

■ Text transfers quickly to your computer. This lets you start reading the text on a page right away. Graphics transfer more slowly. You may have to wait a while to clearly view any graphics.

Tip

If you select a link and nothing happens after several minutes, stop loading the page and try again later.

Note: To stop loading a page, refer to page 22.

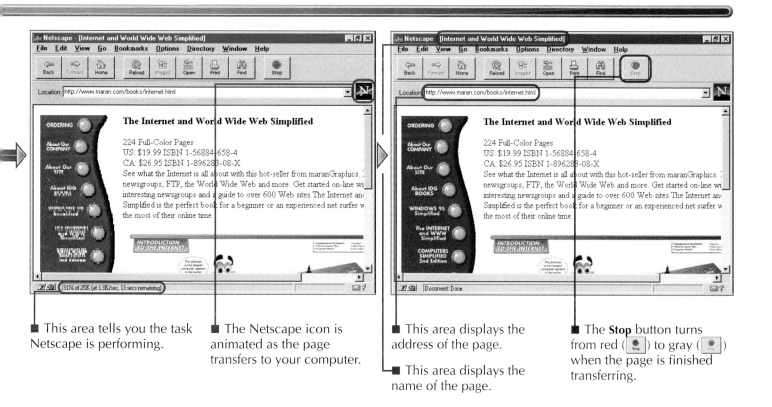

■ This area tells you the task Netscape is performing.

■ The Netscape icon is animated as the page transfers to your computer.

■ This area displays the address of the page.

■ This area displays the name of the page.

■ The **Stop** button turns from red ( ) to gray ( ) when the page is finished transferring.

If a page is taking a long time to transfer to your computer, you can stop loading the page and try connecting again later.

STOP LOADING A PAGE

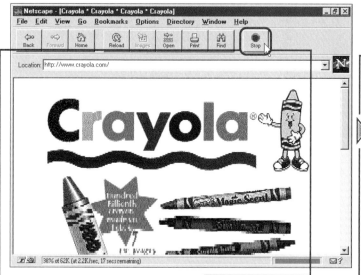

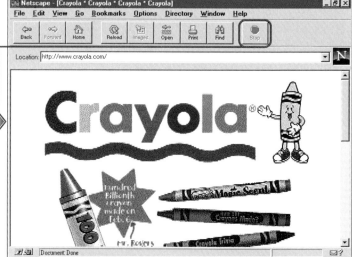

■ The **Stop** button is red ( ) when Netscape is communicating with another computer.

1 To stop the transfer of information, move the mouse over ( ) and then press the left button.

■ The **Stop** button turns gray ( ). This tells you that Netscape is no longer transferring information.

SCROLL THROUGH A PAGE

The scroll bar lets you browse through information on a page.

SCROLL THROUGH A PAGE

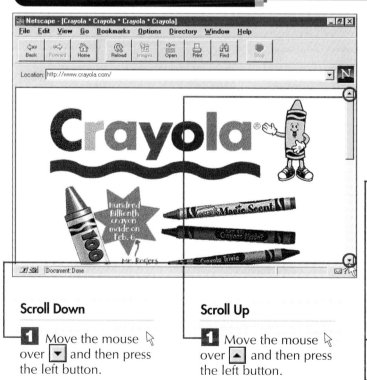

Scroll Down

1 Move the mouse over ▼ and then press the left button.

Scroll Up

1 Move the mouse over ▲ and then press the left button.

Scroll To Any Location

1 Move the mouse over the scroll box.

2 Press and hold down the left button as you drag the scroll box up or down the scroll bar. Then release the button.

Note: The location of the scroll box indicates which part of the page you are viewing. For example, to view the middle of the page, drag the scroll box half way down the scroll bar.

You can easily move back and forth between pages you have already viewed.

MOVE THROUGH PAGES

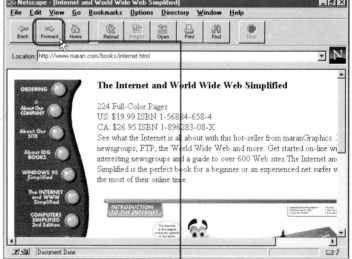

Move Back

1 To return to the last page you viewed, move the mouse ⓘ over [Back] and then press the left button.

■ The last page you viewed appears.

■ To continue to move back through the pages you have viewed, move the mouse ⓘ over [Back] and then press the left button.

Move Forward

1 To move forward through the pages you have viewed, move the mouse ⓘ over [Forward] and then press the left button.

Tips

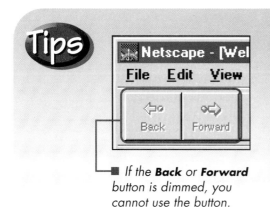

■ If the **Back** or **Forward** button is dimmed, you cannot use the button.

Some Web pages display information in rectangular frames. You cannot use the **Back** or **Forward** buttons to move through pages you have viewed in a frame.

Note: To move through pages you have viewed in a frame, refer to page 26.

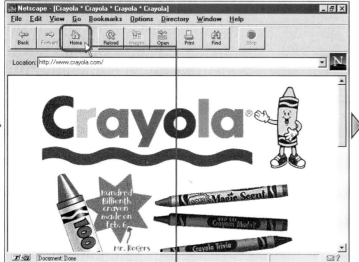

■ The next page appears.

■ To continue to move forward through the pages you have viewed, move the mouse ⅄ over [Forward] and then press the left button.

Return to Home Page

A home page is the first page you see when you start Netscape.

1 To return to your home page, move the mouse ⅄ over [Home] and then press the left button.

■ Your home page appears.

Note: To change your home page, refer to page 64.

USING FRAMES

Some Web pages divide information into rectangular frames. Frames help you move through the information offered by a Web site.

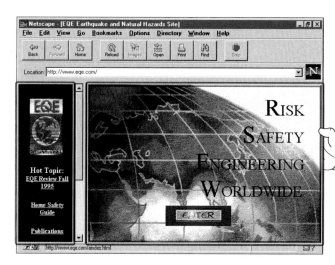

This page displays information in two frames.

USING FRAMES

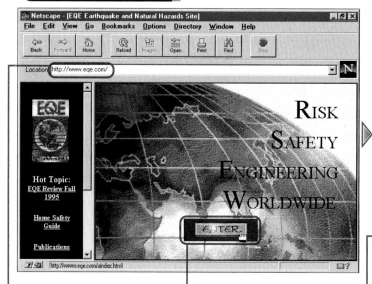

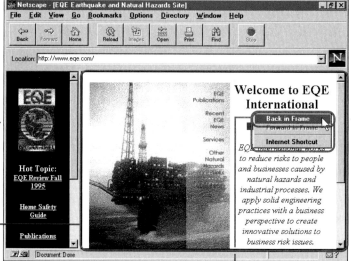

■ In this example, we connect to the page at this address.

Note: To display a Web page, refer to page 18.

Select a Link

1 To select a link in a frame, move the mouse over the highlighted word or picture of interest (changes to 🖑) and then press the left button.

■ The page connected to the item you selected appears.

Move Back in Frame

1 To return to the last page you viewed in a frame, move the mouse over the frame and then press the **right** button. A menu appears.

2 Move the mouse over **Back in Frame** and then press the left button.

- *If the **Back in Frame** or **Forward in Frame** options are dimmed, you cannot use the features.*

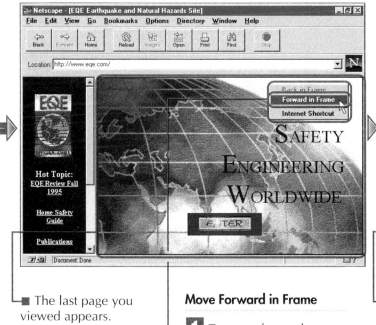

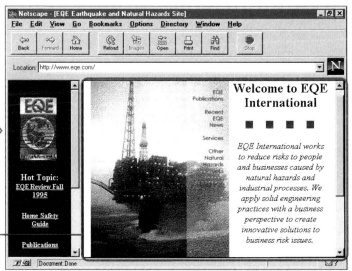

■ The last page you viewed appears.

Move Forward in Frame

1 To move forward through the pages you have viewed in a frame, move the mouse ▷ over the frame and then press the **right** button. A menu appears.

2 Move the mouse ▷ over **Forward in Frame** and then press the left button.

■ The next page appears.

CONNECT TO A SECURE SITE

Netscape lets you know if a Web site you are connecting to is secure. You can safely transfer confidential information to a secure site.

Security is important when you want to send personal information such as credit card numbers or bank records over the Internet.

CONNECT TO A SECURE SITE

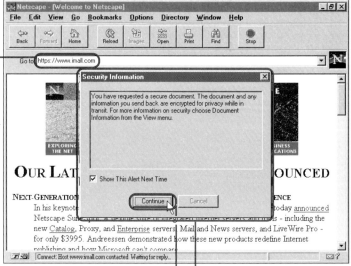

■ When you are at a site that is not secure, the key icon is broken ( ). You cannot safely send confidential information to the site.

■ In this example, we connect to the site at this address. The address of a secure site starts with **https** rather than **http**.

Note: To display a Web page, refer to page 18.

■ This dialog box appears if a site you want to connect to is secure.

1 To close the dialog box, move the mouse over **Continue** and then press the left button.

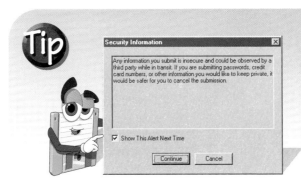

This dialog box appears when information you are about to send over the Internet is not secure. Other people could see any information you send.

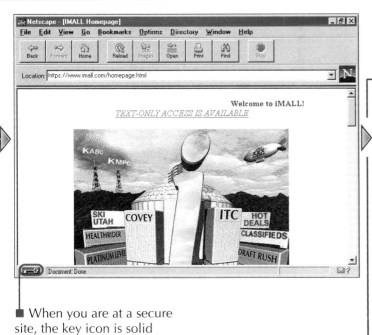

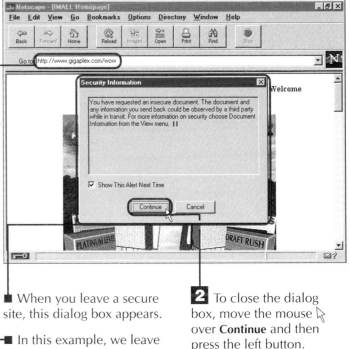

■ When you are at a secure site, the key icon is solid ( ), not broken ( ). You can safely send confidential information to the site.

■ When you leave a secure site, this dialog box appears.

■ In this example, we leave the secure site and connect to the site at this address.

2 To close the dialog box, move the mouse over **Continue** and then press the left button.

If a page appears distorted, you may want to reload the page. Netscape will transfer a fresh copy of the page to your computer.

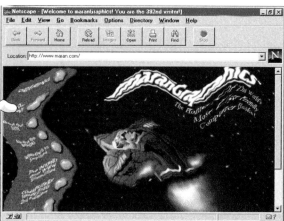

RELOAD A PAGE

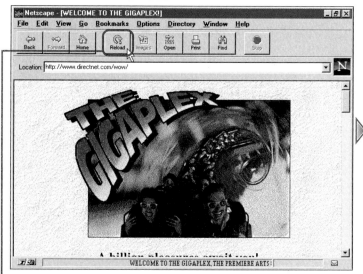

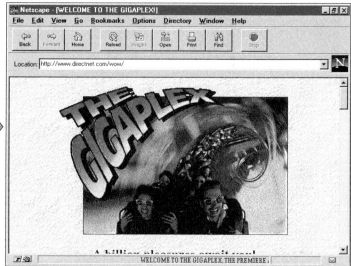

1 Move the mouse over ⟨Reload⟩ and then press the left button.

■ A fresh copy of the page appears on your screen.

Note: You may want to reload a page if you know the information, such as current news, is not up-to-date. Your computer may be displaying an old copy of the page rather than the new one.

CHANGE TOOLBAR APPEARANCE

You can change the way the Toolbar appears on your screen.

Pictures

Text

Pictures and Text

CHANGE TOOLBAR APPEARANCE

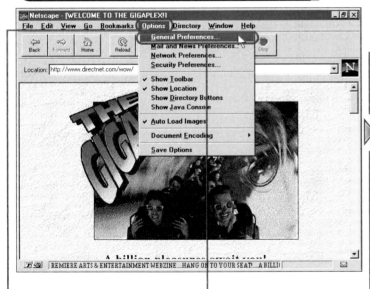

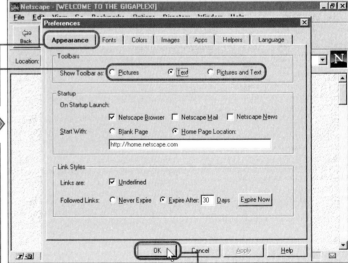

1 Move the mouse over **Options** and then press the left button.

2 Move the mouse over **General Preferences** and then press the left button.

■ The **Preferences** dialog box appears.

3 Move the mouse over the **Appearance** tab and then press the left button.

4 Move the mouse over the way you want the Toolbar to appear and then press the left button (O changes to ⊙).

5 Move the mouse over **OK** and then press the left button.

■ The appearance of the Toolbar changes on your screen.

USING THE DIRECTORY BUTTONS

Netscape offers six buttons to help you quickly access useful and interesting information on the Web.

What's New! | What's Cool! | Handbook | Net Search | Net Directory | Software

USING THE DIRECTORY BUTTONS

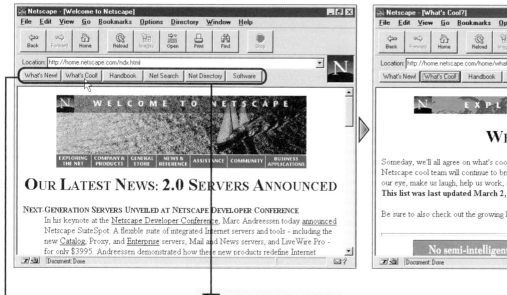

■ This area displays the Directory Buttons.

Note: If the Directory Buttons are not displayed, refer to page 16 to display the buttons.

1 Move the mouse over a button of interest and then press the left button.

■ The Web page for the button you selected appears.

THE DIRECTORY BUTTONS

What's New!

A list of the best new Web sites.

What's Cool!

A list of fun and interesting Web sites, selected by Netscape.

Handbook

An online information manual to help you use Netscape features.

Net Search

A list of Web sites that help you find information on the Web. These sites let you search by entering a word of interest, such as opera or tennis.

Net Directory

A list of Web sites that help you find information on the Web. These sites let you search by looking through different categories, such as business or hobbies.

Software

Information on how to get the latest version of Netscape for your computer.

ERROR MESSAGES

An error message appears when Netscape cannot properly display a Web page.

When an error message appears on your screen, you can try one of these options.

■ If you typed the Web address, check the address for typing errors.

■ Try connecting to the Web page later. The best time to try is during off-peak hours, such as nights and weekends, when fewer people are using the Internet.

ERROR MESSAGES

403 Forbidden

This error message appears when you try to open a Web page you do not have permission to access. You cannot view the Web page without permission.

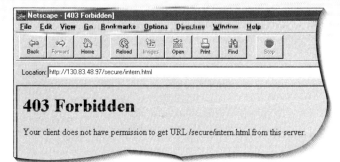

404 Not Found

This error message appears when Netscape cannot find the Web page you specified. The Web page may have moved or changed names.

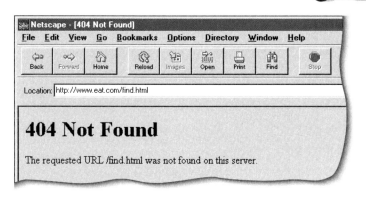

ERROR MESSAGES

ERROR MESSAGES (CONTINUED)

Netscape is unable to use the POP3 server

This error message appears when you try to use Netscape Mail before setting up Mail on your computer.

Note: To set up Mail, refer to page 110.

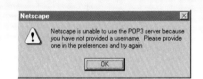

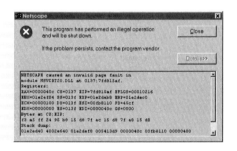

General Protection Fault

This error message appears when Netscape suddenly stops working. To continue, you must exit Netscape and restart the program.

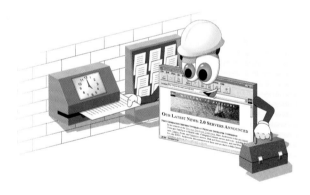

Netscape is unable to locate the server

This error message appears when Netscape cannot find the server you specified. The server may be busy, temporarily not working or may not exist.

Note: A server is a computer that stores information on the Internet.

There was no response

This error message appears when Netscape cannot connect to the server you specified. The server may be busy or temporarily not working.

There was no response... using previously cached copy

This error message appears when Netscape cannot connect to the server you specified, but a copy of the Web page exists in your computer's memory. Netscape will display the Web page, but it may be an old, out-of-date version.

Unknown File Type

This error message appears when Netscape cannot display the graphic or play the sound or video you selected.

Note: You can add programs to your computer to display or play certain types of graphics, sound or video. For more information, refer to page 94.

CHAPTER 3

STORE WEB PAGES

Preview Before Printing

Print a Page

Save a Page or Graphic

Open a Saved Page or Graphic

PREVIEW BEFORE PRINTING

You can see on the screen how a Web page will look when printed.

PREVIEW BEFORE PRINTING

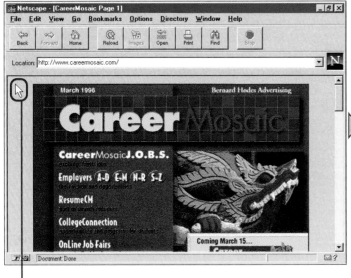

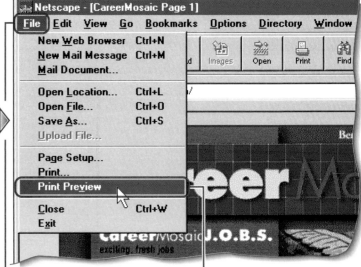

1 Move the mouse ⟍ over a blank area on the page or frame you want to preview and then press the left button.

*Note: For information on frames, refer to the **Tip** on page 41.*

2 Move the mouse ⟍ over **File** and then press the left button.

3 Move the mouse ⟍ over **Print Preview** and then press the left button.

Some Web pages are divided into rectangular frames. If the page displayed on your screen contains frames, you must select the frame you want to preview before printing.

Note: You cannot preview the information in some frames.

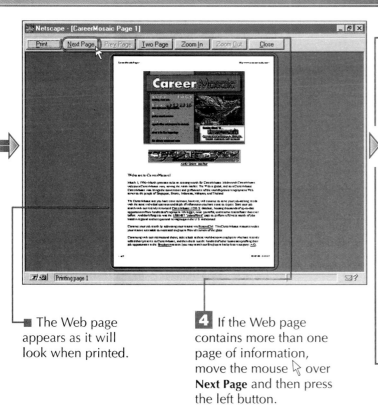

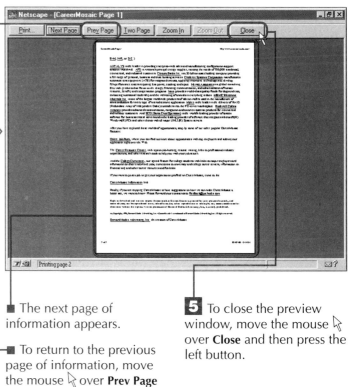

■ The Web page appears as it will look when printed.

4 If the Web page contains more than one page of information, move the mouse ♀ over **Next Page** and then press the left button.

■ The next page of information appears.

■ To return to the previous page of information, move the mouse ♀ over **Prev Page** and then press the left button.

5 To close the preview window, move the mouse ♀ over **Close** and then press the left button.

PRINT A PAGE

You can produce a paper copy of a Web page displayed on your screen. This lets you review the page later on.

PRINT A PAGE

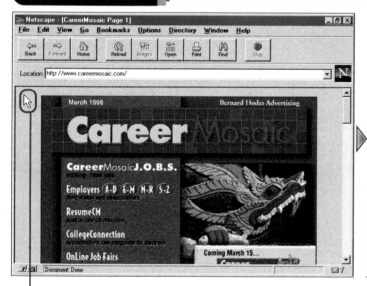

1 Move the mouse ⃞ over a blank area on the page or frame you want to print and then press the left button.

*Note: For information on frames, refer to the **Tip** on page 43.*

2 Move the mouse ⃞ over ⃞ and then press the left button.

Some Web pages are divided into rectangular frames. If the page displayed on your screen contains frames, you must select the frame you want to print.

Note: You cannot print the information in some frames.

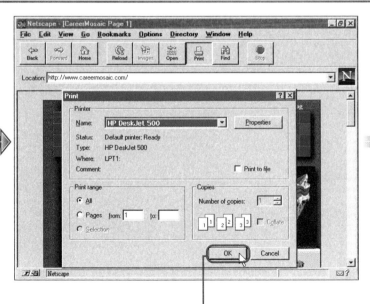

■ The **Print** dialog box appears.

3 Move the mouse over **OK** and then press the left button.

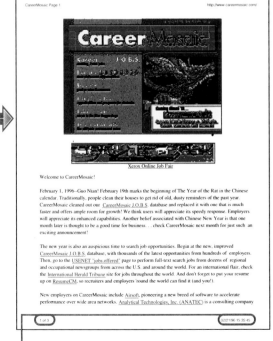

■ Netscape prints the page number and the current date and time on each page.

SAVE A PAGE OR GRAPHIC

You can save a page or graphic displayed on your screen. This lets you view the page or graphic when you are not connected to the Internet.

SAVE A PAGE

1 Move the mouse ▷ over a blank area on the page or frame you want to save and then press the left button.

*Note: For information on frames, refer to the **Tip** on page 45.*

2 Move the mouse ▷ over **File** and then press the left button.

3 Move the mouse ▷ over **Save As** or **Save Frame As** and then press the left button.

■ The **Save As** dialog box appears.

4 This area may display the name of the page or frame. To save the page or frame with a different name, type a new name.

5 Move the mouse ▷ over **Save** and then press the left button.

Note: When you save a page, Netscape only saves the text. When you open a saved page, the graphics will not appear.

Some Web pages are divided into rectangular frames. If the page displayed on your screen uses frames, you must select the frame containing the information you want to save.

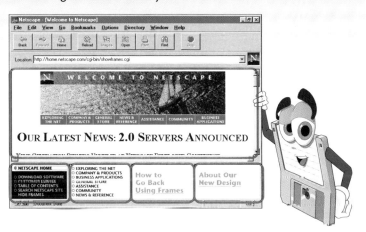

SAVE A GRAPHIC

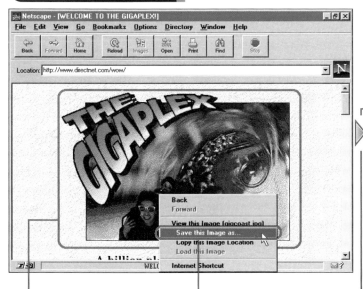

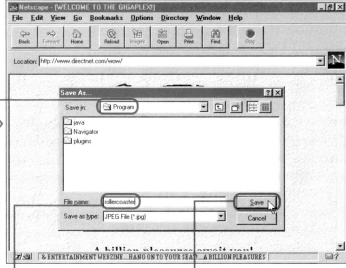

1 Move the mouse (↕ or ⊕) over the graphic you want to save and then press the **right** button. A menu appears.

2 Move the mouse ↕ over **Save this Image as** and then press the left button.

■ The **Save As** dialog box appears.

3 This area displays the name of the graphic. To save the graphic with a different name, type a new name.

■ This area displays the location where the graphic will be stored.

4 Move the mouse ↕ over **Save** and then press the left button.

You can open and view a page or graphic you previously saved.

OPEN A SAVED PAGE OR GRAPHIC

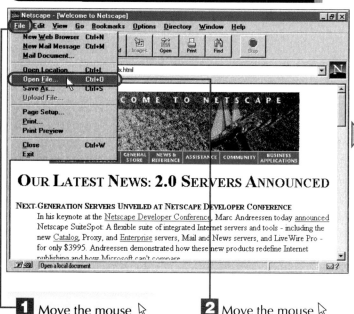

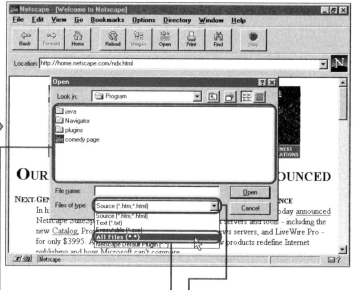

1 Move the mouse � over **File** and then press the left button.

2 Move the mouse � over **Open File** and then press the left button.

■ The **Open** dialog box appears.

■ This area displays the names of all the pages you have saved.

3 To display the names of everything you have saved in Netscape, move the mouse � over this area and then press the left button.

4 Move the mouse � over **All Files** and then press the left button.

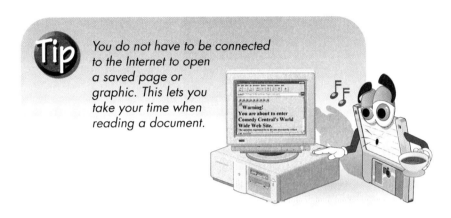

Tip

You do not have to be connected to the Internet to open a saved page or graphic. This lets you take your time when reading a document.

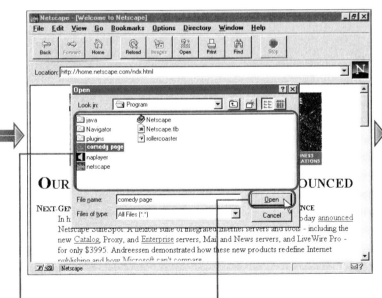

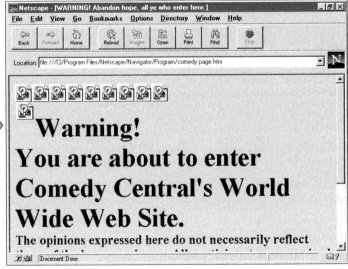

■ This area now displays the names of everything you have saved in Netscape.

5 Move the mouse ▷ over the item you want to open and then press the left button.

6 Move the mouse ▷ over **Open** and then press the left button.

■ The item you selected appears on your screen.

Note: When you save a page, Netscape only saves the text. When you open a saved page, the graphics will not appear.

TIME-SAVING FEATURES

 Display History of Viewed Pages

 Using Bookmarks

 Manage Bookmarks

 Find Text on a Page

 Turn Off Graphics

 Change Your Home Page

 Open a New Netscape Window

 Change Startup Window

Netscape keeps track of all the pages you have viewed since you started the program. You can instantly return to any of these pages.

Comedy Central : http://www.comcentral.com
maranGraphics : http://www.maran.com
CareerMosaic : http://www.careermos.a...
IMALL : http://www.imall.c...
GigaPlex : http://www.direct.com

DISPLAY HISTORY OF VIEWED PAGES

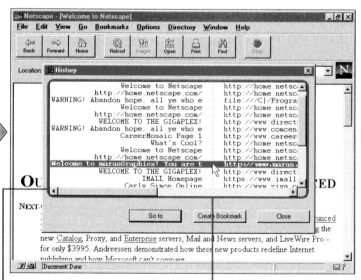

1 Move the mouse over **Window** and then press the left button.

2 Move the mouse over **History** and then press the left button.

■ The **History** dialog box appears.

■ This area displays the name and address of each page you have viewed since you started Netscape.

Note: The pages you viewed most recently appear at the top of the list.

3 Move the mouse over the name of the page you want to view again and then press the left button.

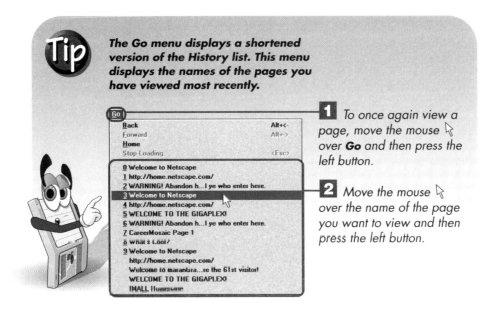

Tip

The Go menu displays a shortened version of the History list. This menu displays the names of the pages you have viewed most recently.

1 To once again view a page, move the mouse ⌖ over **Go** and then press the left button.

2 Move the mouse ⌖ over the name of the page you want to view and then press the left button.

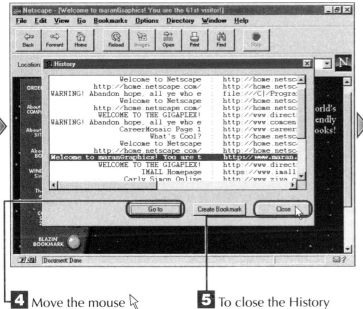

4 Move the mouse ⌖ over **Go to** and then press the left button.

5 To close the History dialog box, move the mouse ⌖ over **Close** and then press the left button.

■ The page you selected appears.

USING BOOKMARKS

Like a bookmark that holds your place in a novel, Netscape bookmarks let you quickly return to your favorite pages on the Web.

ADD A BOOKMARK

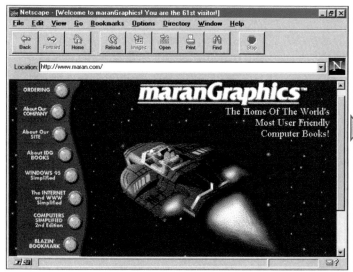

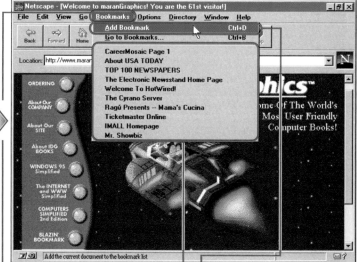

■ You can add the page displayed on your screen to your list of bookmarks.

1 Move the mouse ℞ over **Bookmarks** and then press the left button.

2 Move the mouse ℞ over **Add Bookmark** and then press the left button.

■ Netscape will add the page to your list of bookmarks.

Tip

Netscape remembers the pages you marked with bookmarks, even when you exit the program. The next time you start Netscape, you can quickly view any bookmarked page.

VIEW A BOOKMARKED PAGE

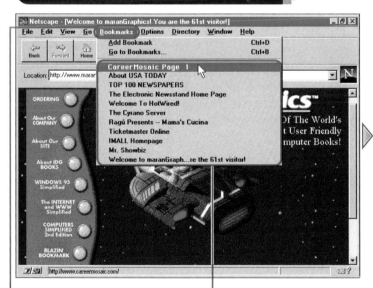

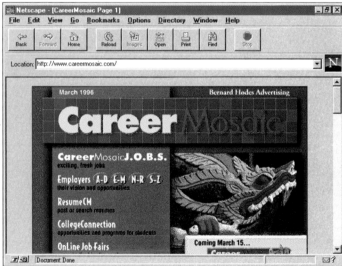

1 To view a bookmarked page, move the mouse over **Bookmarks** and then press the left button.

■ This area displays a list of all your bookmarked pages.

2 Move the mouse over the name of the page you want to view and then press the left button.

■ The page you selected appears.

MANAGE BOOKMARKS

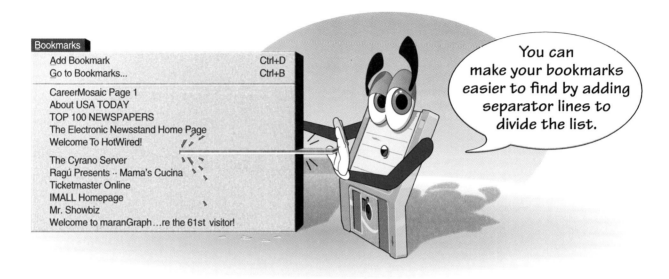

Bookmarks

Add Bookmark   Ctrl+D
Go to Bookmarks...   Ctrl+B

CareerMosaic Page 1
About USA TODAY
TOP 100 NEWSPAPERS
The Electronic Newsstand Home Page
Welcome To HotWired!

The Cyrano Server
Ragú Presents -- Mama's Cucina
Ticketmaster Online
IMALL Homepage
Mr. Showbiz
Welcome to maranGraph...re the 61st visitor!

> You can make your bookmarks easier to find by adding separator lines to divide the list.

ADD A SEPARATOR LINE

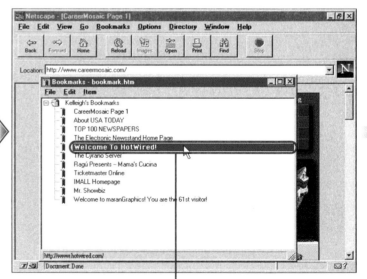

1 Move the mouse over **Bookmarks** and then press the left button.

2 Move the mouse over **Go to Bookmarks** and then press the left button.

■ The **Bookmarks** window appears, displaying a list of your bookmarks.

■ When you add a separator line, the line will appear below the bookmark you select.

3 To select a bookmark, move the mouse over the bookmark and then press the left button.

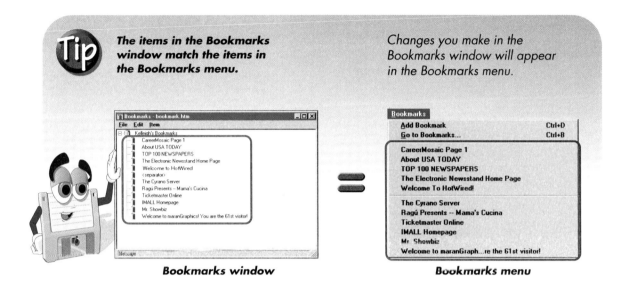

Tip

The items in the Bookmarks window match the items in the Bookmarks menu.

Changes you make in the Bookmarks window will appear in the Bookmarks menu.

Bookmarks window

Bookmarks menu

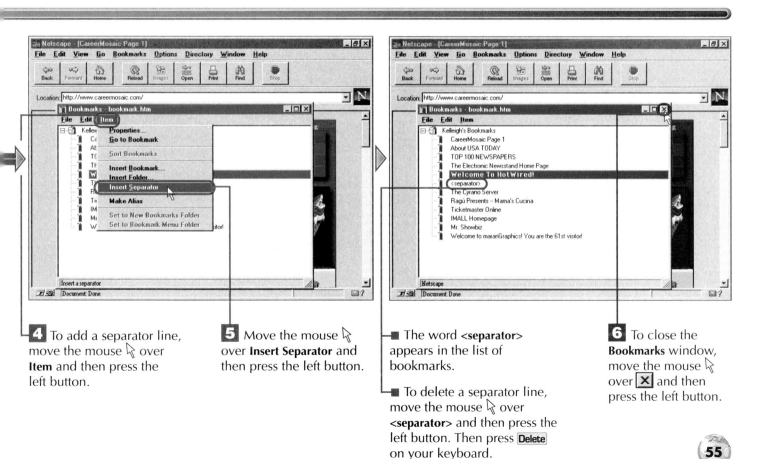

4 To add a separator line, move the mouse ⬡ over **Item** and then press the left button.

5 Move the mouse ⬡ over **Insert Separator** and then press the left button.

■ The word **<separator>** appears in the list of bookmarks.

■ To delete a separator line, move the mouse ⬡ over **<separator>** and then press the left button. Then press **Delete** on your keyboard.

6 To close the **Bookmarks** window, move the mouse ⬡ over **X** and then press the left button.

MANAGE BOOKMARKS

You can create a folder to place related bookmarks together.

CREATE A BOOKMARK FOLDER

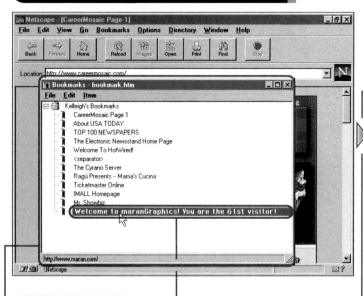

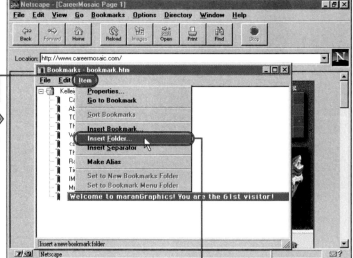

1 To display the **Bookmarks** window, perform steps **1** and **2** on page 54.

■ When you create a folder, the folder will appear below the bookmark you select.

2 To select a bookmark, move the mouse ⇖ over the bookmark and then press the left button.

3 To create a folder, move the mouse ⇖ over **Item** and then press the left button.

4 Move the mouse ⇖ over **Insert Folder** and then press the left button.

■ The **Bookmark Properties** dialog box appears.

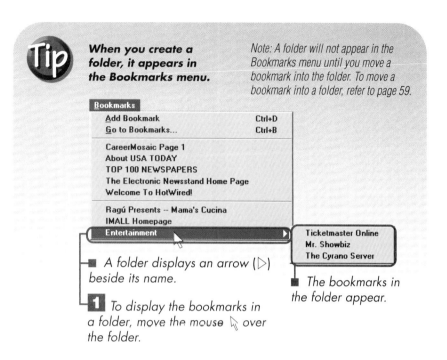

Tip

When you create a folder, it appears in the Bookmarks menu.

Note: A folder will not appear in the Bookmarks menu until you move a bookmark into the folder. To move a bookmark into a folder, refer to page 59.

■ *A folder displays an arrow (▷) beside its name.*

1 *To display the bookmarks in a folder, move the mouse ↳ over the folder.*

■ *The bookmarks in the folder appear.*

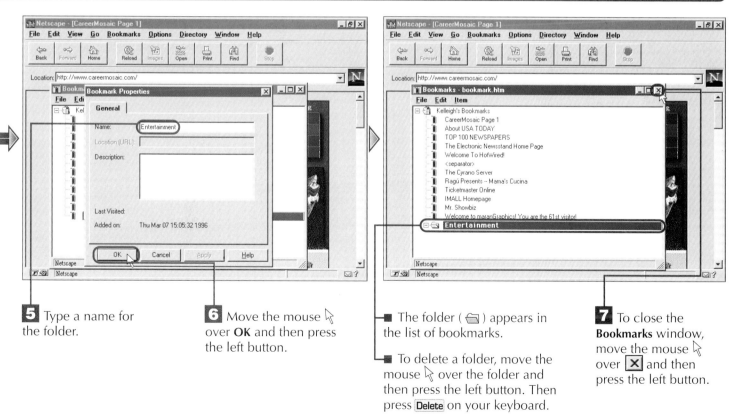

5 Type a name for the folder.

6 Move the mouse ↳ over **OK** and then press the left button.

■ The folder (🗀) appears in the list of bookmarks.

■ To delete a folder, move the mouse ↳ over the folder and then press the left button. Then press **Delete** on your keyboard.

Note: When you delete a folder, any bookmarks in the folder will also be deleted.

7 To close the **Bookmarks** window, move the mouse ↳ over **X** and then press the left button.

MANAGE BOOKMARKS

You can delete a bookmark you no longer need.

DELETE A BOOKMARK

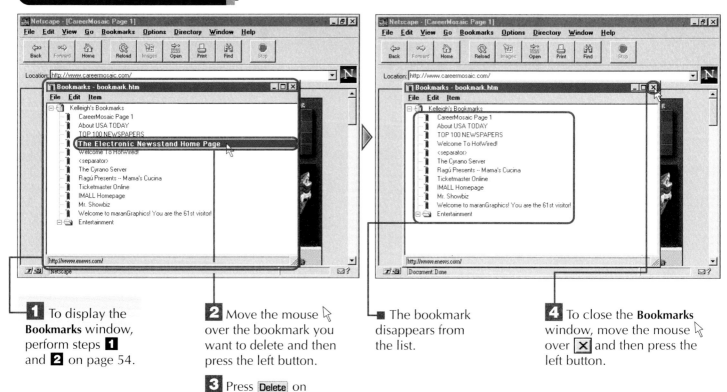

1 To display the **Bookmarks** window, perform steps **1** and **2** on page 54.

2 Move the mouse ⌖ over the bookmark you want to delete and then press the left button.

3 Press **Delete** on your keyboard.

■ The bookmark disappears from the list.

4 To close the **Bookmarks** window, move the mouse ⌖ over **X** and then press the left button.

You can easily rearrange the bookmarks in your list.

MOVE A BOOKMARK

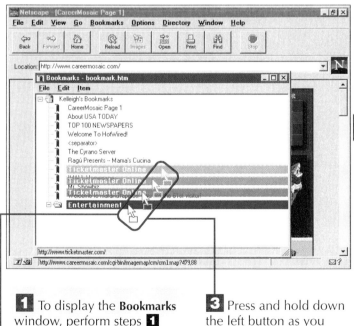

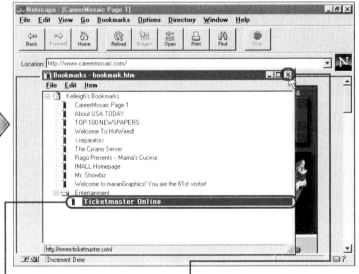

1 To display the **Bookmarks** window, perform steps **1** and **2** on page 54.

2 Position the mouse ☝ over the bookmark you want to move.

3 Press and hold down the left button as you move the mouse ☝ to the new location. Then release the button.

Note: The bookmark will appear in the folder (🗀) you highlight or below the bookmark (🔖) you highlight.

■ The bookmark appears in the new location.

Note: In this example, we move the bookmark into a folder.

4 To close the **Bookmarks** window, move the mouse ☝ over **X** and then press the left button.

If you are viewing a page that contains a lot of text, you can use the Find feature to quickly locate a specific word.

FIND TEXT ON A PAGE

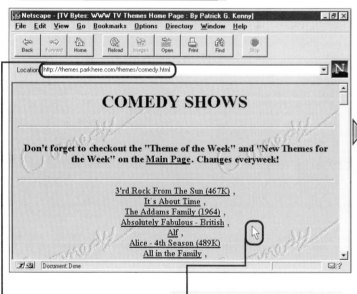

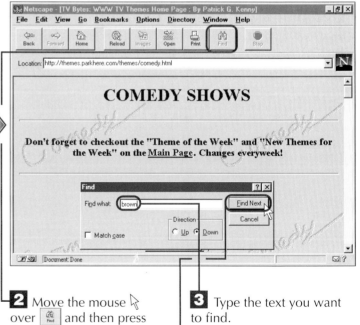

■ In this example, we connect to the page at this address.

Note: To display a Web page, refer to page 18.

1 Move the mouse ⟍ over a blank area on the page or frame containing the text you want to find and then press the left button.

*Note: For information on frames, refer to the **Tip** on page 61.*

2 Move the mouse ⟍ over 🔍 and then press the left button.

■ The **Find** dialog box appears.

3 Type the text you want to find.

4 Move the mouse ⟍ over **Find Next** and then press the left button.

Tip Some Web pages are divided into rectangular frames. If the page displayed on your screen contains frames, you must select the frame containing the text you want to find.

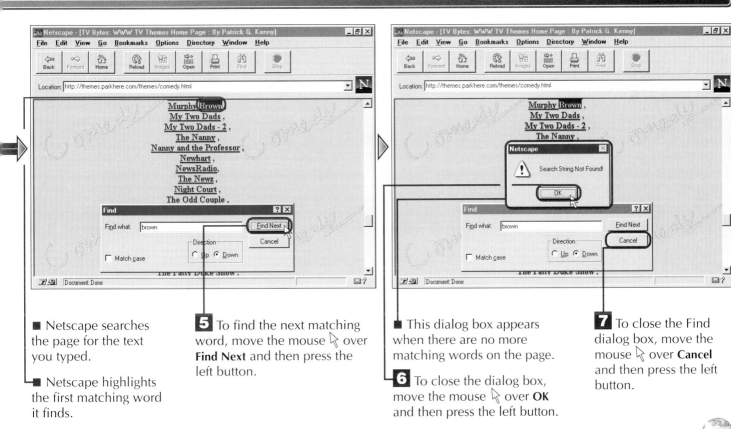

■ Netscape searches the page for the text you typed.

■ Netscape highlights the first matching word it finds.

5 To find the next matching word, move the mouse over **Find Next** and then press the left button.

■ This dialog box appears when there are no more matching words on the page.

6 To close the dialog box, move the mouse over **OK** and then press the left button.

7 To close the Find dialog box, move the mouse over **Cancel** and then press the left button.

TURN OFF GRAPHICS

Graphics can take a long time to transfer to your computer. Although graphics can make pages attractive, you can save time by turning off the display of graphics.

TURN OFF GRAPHICS

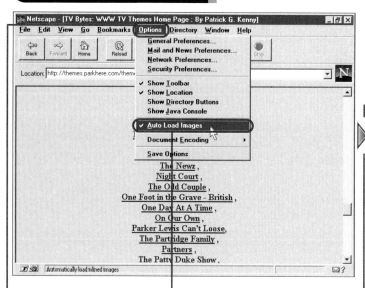

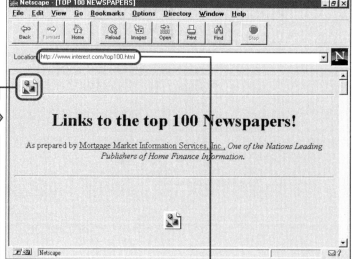

1 Move the mouse ▹ over **Options** and then press the left button.

■ A check mark (✔) beside this option tells you that Netscape will display graphics.

2 To turn off the display of graphics, move the mouse ▹ over **Auto Load Images** and then press the left button.

■ The next time you connect to a page on the Web, small icons appear where graphics usually appear.

■ In this example, we connect to the page at this address.

Note: To display a Web page, refer to page 18.

Tip

A graphic can be a picture, fancy character or small icon.

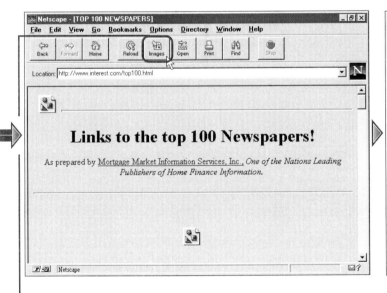

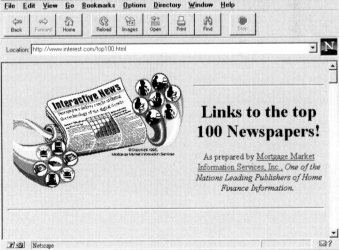

3 To display all the graphics on the page, move the mouse over 🖼 and then press the left button.

■ All the graphics appear.

Turn On Graphics

1 To display graphics on all future pages, repeat steps **1** and **2** on page 62.

CHANGE YOUR HOME PAGE

You can select which page you want to appear each time you start Netscape.

CHANGE YOUR HOME PAGE

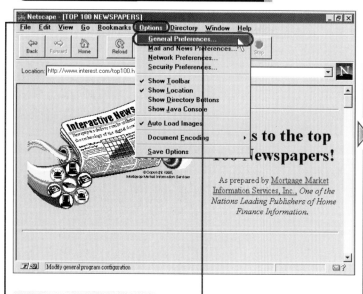

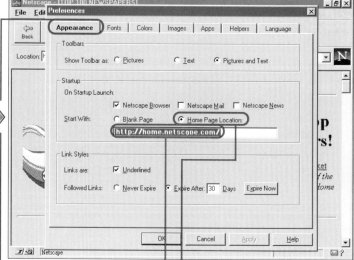

1 Move the mouse ⍈ over **Options** and then press the left button.

2 Move the mouse ⍈ over **General Preferences** and then press the left button.

■ The **Preferences** dialog box appears.

3 Move the mouse ⍈ over the **Appearance** tab and then press the left button.

4 Move the mouse ⍈ over **Home Page Location:** and then press the left button (○ changes to ◉).

5 Press **Tab** on your keyboard to highlight the text in this area.

Tip

A home page should provide a good starting point for exploring the Web. Choose a home page that will quickly take you to Web pages that interest you.

DISPLAY YOUR HOME PAGE

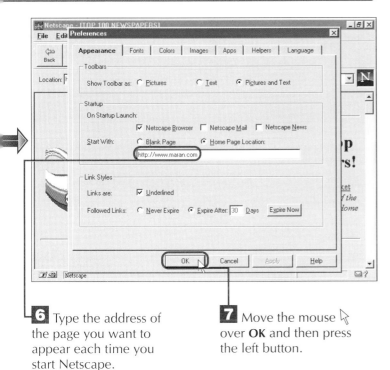

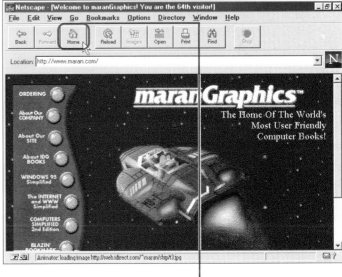

6 Type the address of the page you want to appear each time you start Netscape.

7 Move the mouse ▷ over **OK** and then press the left button.

You can display your home page at any time.

1 Move the mouse ▷ over [Home] and then press the left button.

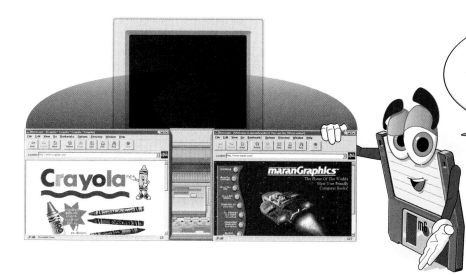

You can open a new Netscape window to display two Web pages at once.

Since there is no connection between the Netscape windows, you can perform completely separate tasks in each window.

OPEN A NEW NETSCAPE WINDOW

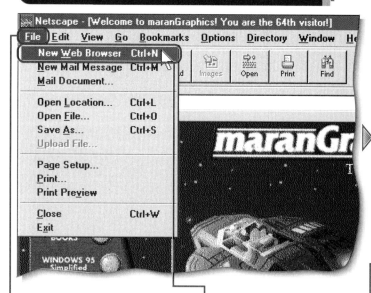

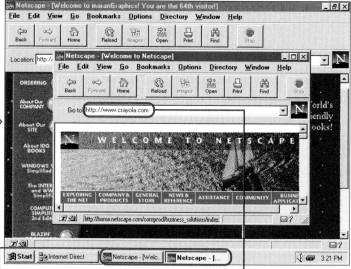

1 Move the mouse ⟍ over **File** and then press the left button.

2 Move the mouse ⟍ over **New Web Browser** and then press the left button.

■ A new Netscape window appears.

■ The taskbar displays a button for each Netscape window.

■ To move the Netscape window you want to work with to the front, move the mouse ⟍ over its button on the taskbar and then press the left button.

3 To display another Web page in the Netscape window, move the mouse I over this area and then press the left button. Then type the address of the page you want to view and press **Enter** on your keyboard.

Tip

Opening a new Netscape window is very useful when a page is taking a long time to transfer to your computer. You can open a new Netscape window and view a different page while you are waiting.

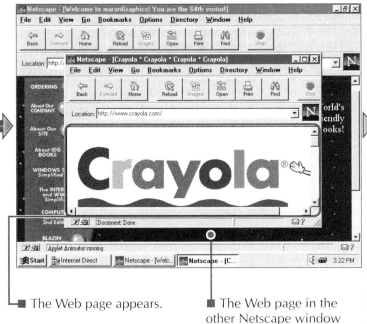

■ The Web page appears.

■ The Web page in the other Netscape window does not change.

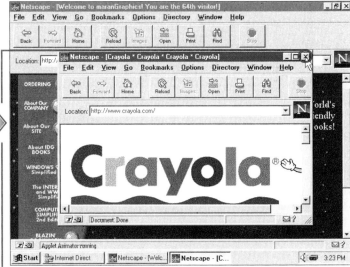

Close a Netscape Window

1 To close a Netscape window and remove it from your screen, move the mouse ⊹ over X in the window and then press the left button.

Netscape consists of three main windows. You can specify which window you want to appear each time you start Netscape.

Netscape Browser
Lets you browse through the information on the Internet.

CHANGE STARTUP WINDOW

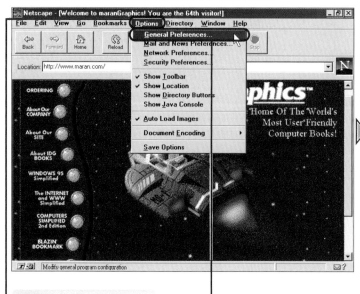

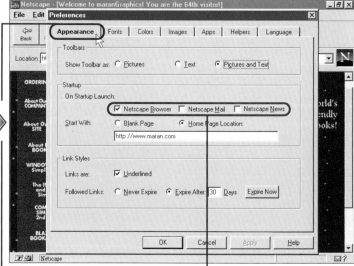

1 Move the mouse over **Options** and then press the left button.

2 Move the mouse over **General Preferences** and then press the left button.

■ The **Preferences** dialog box appears.

3 Move the mouse over the **Appearance** tab and then press the left button.

■ This area displays the three windows that Netscape can open automatically each time you start the program.

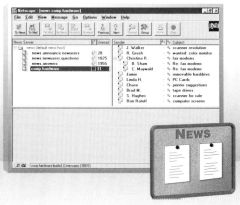

Netscape Mail
Lets you send and receive
electronic messages.

*Note: For information on Netscape Mail,
refer to page 108.*

Netscape News
Lets you read and post
newsgroup articles.

*Note: For information on Netscape News,
refer to page 164.*

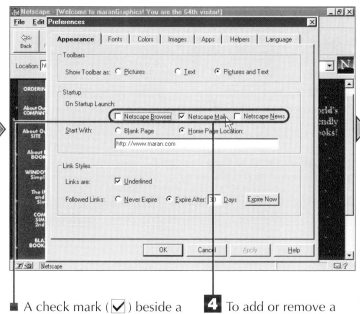

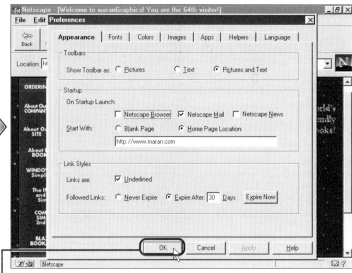

■ A check mark (✓) beside a
window shows that the window
will open automatically each
time you start Netscape.

*Note: You can have more than one
window open automatically each
time you start Netscape.*

4 To add or remove a
check mark (✓), move
the mouse ⇗ over a
window and then press
the left button.

■ Repeat step **4** for all
the check marks you want
to add or remove.

5 To confirm the changes,
move the mouse ⇗ over **OK**
and then press the left
button.

CHAPTER

SEARCH THE WEB

 Yahoo

 Lycos

 Point

 Alta Vista

 Deja News

 WhoWhere?

YAHOO

Yahoo is a free service that helps you find information on the Web. You can browse through Yahoo's categories to find information that interests you.

YAHOO (SEARCH BY CATEGORY)

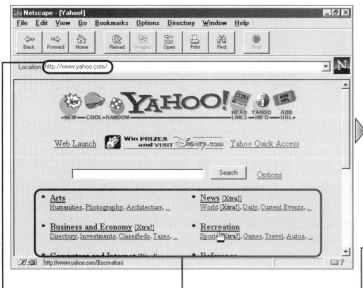

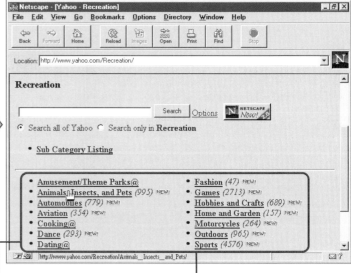

1 To display the Yahoo page, move the mouse I over this area and then press the left button.

2 Type **http://www.yahoo.com** and then press **Enter** on your keyboard.

■ This area displays a list of the main Yahoo categories.

Note: To view all the categories, use the scroll bar. For more information, refer to page 23.

3 Move the mouse 🖑 over a category of interest and then press the left button.

■ A list of subcategories appears.

■ The number in brackets beside a subcategory shows how many Web pages are in the subcategory.

4 Move the mouse 🖑 over a subcategory of interest and then press the left button.

5 Repeat step **4** until you see a list of Web pages that interest you.

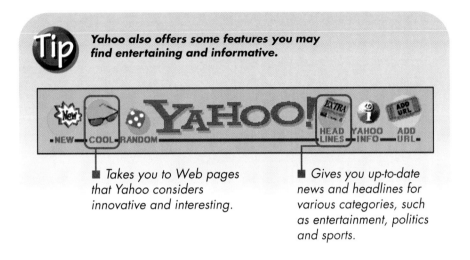

Tip

Yahoo also offers some features you may find entertaining and informative.

■ *Takes you to Web pages that Yahoo considers innovative and interesting.*

■ *Gives you up-to-date news and headlines for various categories, such as entertainment, politics and sports.*

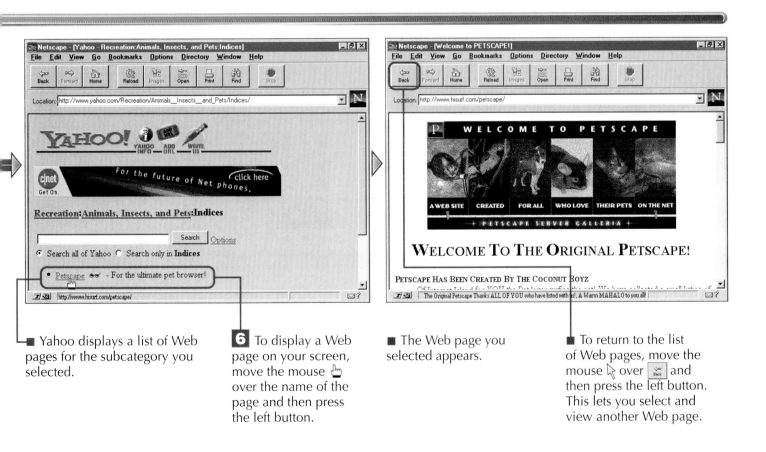

■ Yahoo displays a list of Web pages for the subcategory you selected.

6 To display a Web page on your screen, move the mouse 👆 over the name of the page and then press the left button.

■ The Web page you selected appears.

■ To return to the list of Web pages, move the mouse ⬚ over Back and then press the left button. This lets you select and view another Web page.

YAHOO

> You can quickly find information of interest by searching for a specific topic in Yahoo's list of Web pages.

YAHOO (SEARCH BY WORD)

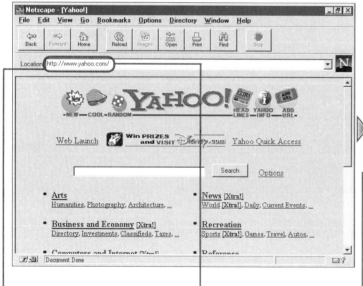

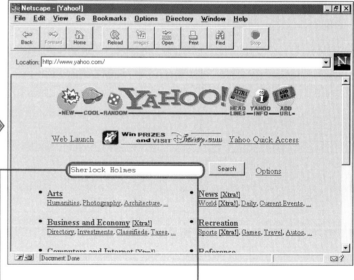

1 To display the Yahoo page, move the mouse I over this area and then press the left button.

2 Type **http://www.yahoo.com** and then press **Enter** on your keyboard.

3 To search for a topic of interest, move the mouse I over this area and then press the left button.

4 Type the topic of interest and then press **Enter** on your keyboard.

Tip

There are two ways Yahoo finds new Web pages.

■ People submit information to Yahoo about pages they have created.

■ Automated robots also travel around the Web looking for new pages.

Since hundreds of new pages are created each day, it is impossible for Yahoo to find and catalog every new page on the Web.

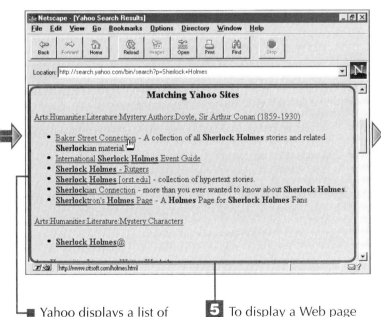

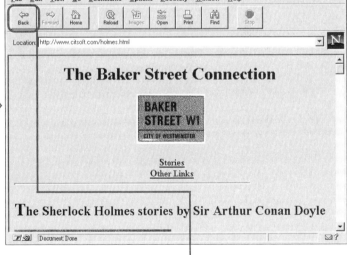

■ Yahoo displays a list of Web pages containing the topic you specified. Each page displays a dot (●) beside its name.

Note: To view the list, use the scroll bar. For more information, refer to page 23.

5 To display a Web page on your screen, move the mouse 🖑 over the name of the page and then press the left button.

■ The Web page you selected appears.

■ To return to the list of Web pages, move the mouse ⌖ over [Back] and then press the left button. This lets you select and view another Web page.

LYCOS

Lycos catalogs millions of Web pages to help you quickly find information of interest.

Lycos comes from the first five letters of the Latin name for Wolf Spider.

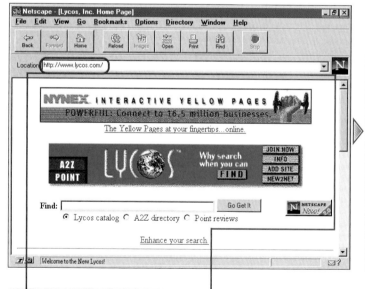

1 To display the Lycos page, move the mouse I over this area and then press the left button.

2 Type **http://www.lycos.com** and then press **Enter** on your keyboard.

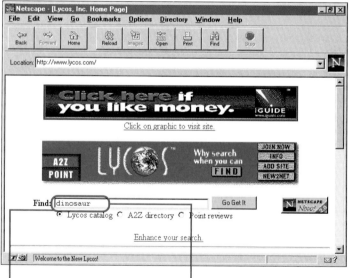

3 To search for a topic of interest, move the mouse I over this area and then press the left button.

4 Type the topic of interest and then press **Enter** on your keyboard.

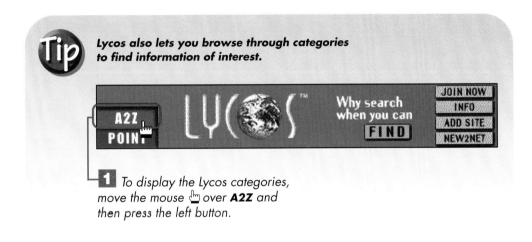

Tip

Lycos also lets you browse through categories to find information of interest.

1 To display the Lycos categories, move the mouse over **A2Z** and then press the left button.

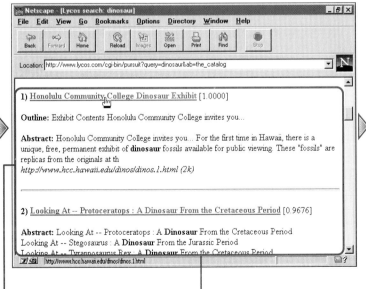

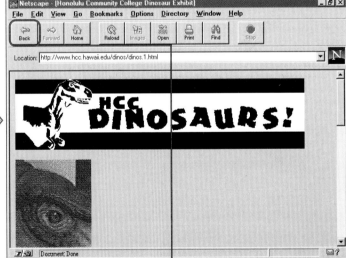

■ A list of the top ten Web pages containing the topic you specified appears.

Note: To view the list, use the scroll bar. For more information, refer to page 23.

5 To display a Web page on your screen, move the mouse over the name of the page and then press the left button.

■ The Web page you selected appears.

■ To return to the list of Web pages, move the mouse over and then press the left button. This lets you select and view another Web page.

Point keeps track of the best pages on the Web. You can search this listing to find Web pages for a topic of interest.

POINT

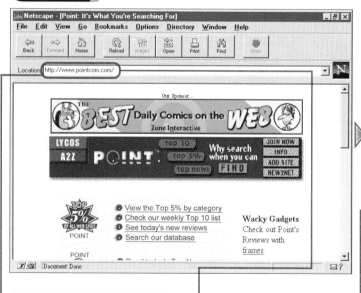

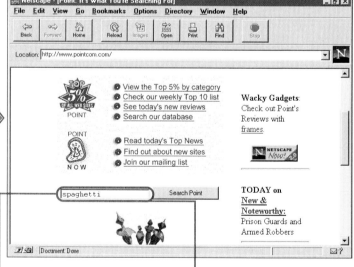

1 To display the Point page, move the mouse I over this area and then press the left button.

2 Type **http://www.pointcom.com** and then press **Enter** on your keyboard.

3 To search for a word of interest, move the mouse I over this area and then press the left button.

4 Type the word of interest and then press **Enter** on your keyboard.

Note: To display the area, use the scroll bar. For more information, refer to page 23.

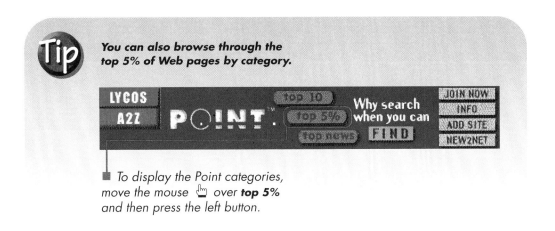

Tip

You can also browse through the top 5% of Web pages by category.

■ To display the Point categories, move the mouse over **top 5%** and then press the left button.

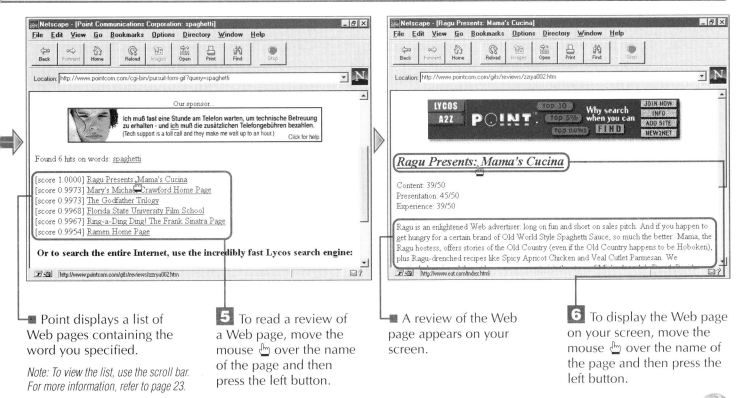

■ Point displays a list of Web pages containing the word you specified.

Note: To view the list, use the scroll bar. For more information, refer to page 23.

5 To read a review of a Web page, move the mouse over the name of the page and then press the left button.

■ A review of the Web page appears on your screen.

6 To display the Web page on your screen, move the mouse over the name of the page and then press the left button.

Alta Vista
lets you search
Web pages or newsgroup
articles for a topic
of interest.

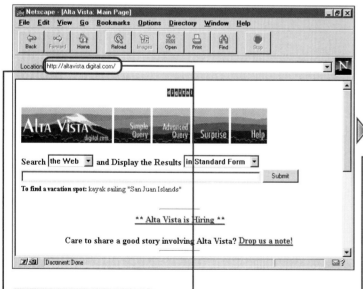

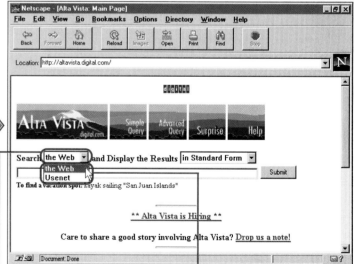

1 To display the Alta Vista page, move the mouse I over this area and then press the left button.

2 Type **http://altavista.digital.com** and then press **Enter** on your keyboard.

3 To specify whether you want to search Web pages or newsgroup articles, move the mouse ⟨ over this area and then press the left button.

4 Move the mouse ⟨ over one of the following options and then press the left button.

the Web - Searches Web pages.

Usenet - Searches newsgroup articles.

Tip

A newsgroup is a discussion group on the Internet that allows people with similar interests to communicate. There are thousands of newsgroups on every subject imaginable.

Note: For more information on newsgroups, refer to page 160.

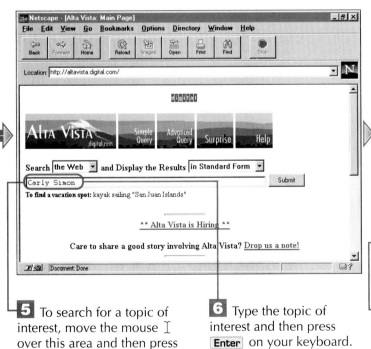

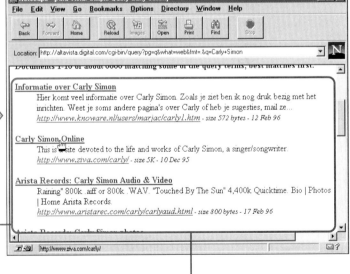

5 To search for a topic of interest, move the mouse I over this area and then press the left button.

6 Type the topic of interest and then press Enter on your keyboard.

■ A list of Web pages or newsgroup articles containing the topic you specified appears.

Note: To view the list, use the scroll bar. For more information, refer to page 23.

7 To display a Web page or newsgroup article on your screen, move the mouse 🖑 over the name of the item and then press the left button.

Deja News lets you search newsgroup articles for a topic of interest.

For information on newsgroups, refer to page 160.

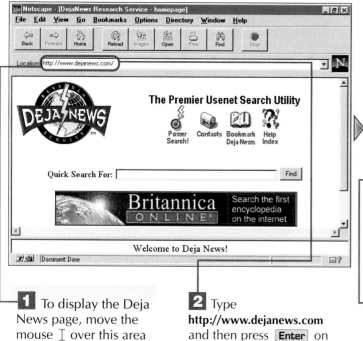

1 To display the Deja News page, move the mouse I over this area and then press the left button.

2 Type **http://www.dejanews.com** and then press **Enter** on your keyboard.

3 To search for a topic of interest, move the mouse I over this area and then press the left button.

4 Type the topic of interest and then press **Enter** on your keyboard.

*Note: If the **Security Information** dialog box appears, move the mouse over **Continue** and then press the left button to close the dialog box.*

Tip

If you plan to use Deja News often, you can create a bookmark for the page. This lets you quickly return to Deja News at any time.

Note: To create a bookmark, refer to page 52.

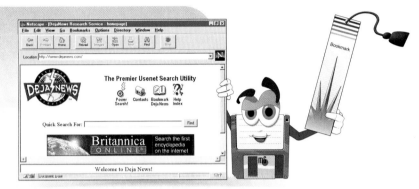

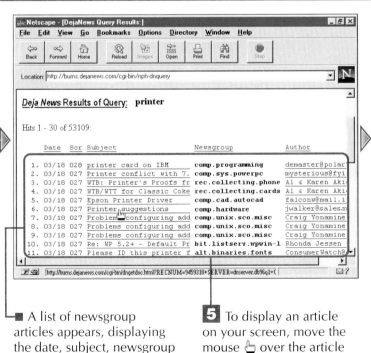

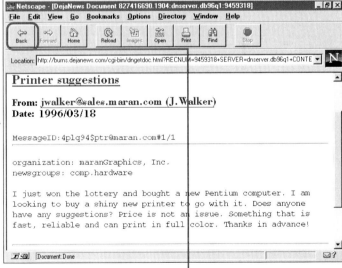

■ A list of newsgroup articles appears, displaying the date, subject, newsgroup and author of each article that contains the topic you specified.

Note: To view the list, use the scroll bar. For more information, refer to page 23.

5 To display an article on your screen, move the mouse 🖑 over the article and then press the left button.

■ The article you selected appears.

■ To return to the list of articles, move the mouse over [Back] and then press the left button. This lets you select and view another article.

WhoWhere? can help you find the e-mail address of a friend or colleague.

When you find the e-mail address of a friend or colleague, you can send them an electronic message. For information on e-mail, refer to page 104.

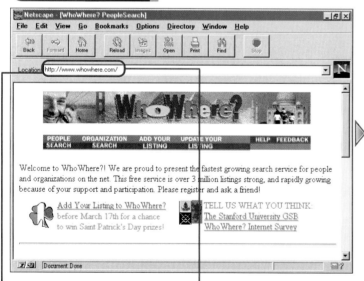

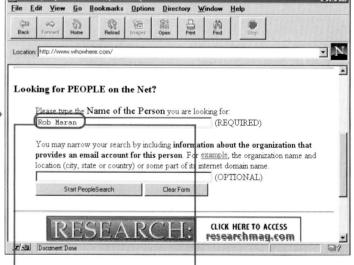

1 To display the WhoWhere? page, move the mouse I over this area and then press the left button.

2 Type **http://www.whowhere.com** and then press **Enter** on your keyboard.

3 Move the mouse I over this area and then press the left button.

Note: To display the area, use the scroll bar. For more information, refer to page 23.

4 Type the name of the person you are looking for.

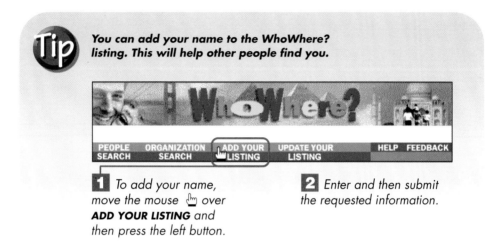

Tip

You can add your name to the WhoWhere? listing. This will help other people find you.

1 To add your name, move the mouse 🖑 over **ADD YOUR LISTING** and then press the left button.

2 Enter and then submit the requested information.

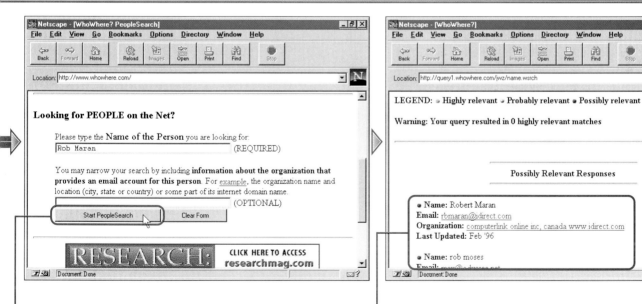

5 To start the search, move the mouse ▷ over **Start PeopleSearch** and then press the left button.

*Note: If the **Security Information** dialog box appears, move the mouse ▷ over **Continue** and then press the left button to close the dialog box.*

■ A list appears, displaying the name and e-mail address of each person who matches the name you specified.

Note: To view the list, use the scroll bar. For more information, refer to page 23.

CHAPTER 6

In this chapter you will learn how to display or play graphics, sound and video on your computer.

MULTIMEDIA ON THE WEB

 Introduction

 Java and JavaScript

 Play Sounds

 Plug-Ins

INTRODUCTION

Web pages can include an exciting combination of text, graphics, sound and video.

TYPES OF FILES

Netscape looks at the last few characters in a file name, called the extension, to determine how to display or play a file on a Web page. For example, **gif** in the file name **porsche.gif** tells Netscape that the file is a graphics file.

Netscape needs special programs, called plug-ins, to display or play certain types of graphics, sound and video on the Web.

Note: For information on plug-ins, refer to page 94.

letter.txt

Text

Netscape can display text files with the htm, html, text or txt extension.

music.au

Sound

Netscape can play sound files with the aif, aifc, aiff, au or snd extension.

porsche.gif

Graphics

Netscape can display graphics files with the gif, jpe, jpeg, jpg or xbm extension.

preview.vdo

Video

Netscape does not come with the capability to play video files.

Sound and video files can take time to transfer to your computer.

TIME

	FILES	
Name	Date	Size
bugle.aif	22 Mar 1996	1289 Kb
trumpet.aif	12 Nov 1996	819 Kb
drums.aif	22 Mar 1996	707 Kb
violin.aif	23 Mar 1996	221 Kb
flute.aif	17 Nov 1996	4334 Kb
bach.aif	12 Nov 1996	3461 Kb
horn.aif	10 May 1996	5459 Kb
cello.aif	27 Oct 1996	1211 Kb
canary.aif	30 Nov 1996	9472 Kb
plane.aif	16 May 1996	236 Kb
viola.aif	11 Oct 1996	1442 Kb
bass.aif	30 Nov 1996	2334 Kb
Handel.aif	18 Nov 1996	231 Kb

5459 Kb

A Web page will usually show you the size of a file to give you an indication of how long the file will take to transfer to your computer.

Use this chart as a guide to determine how long the transfer will take.

	File Size		Time
Bytes	Kilobytes (Kb)	Megabytes (Mb)	(estimated)
10,000,000	10,000	10	1 hour
5,000,000	5,000	5	30 minutes
2,500,000	2,500	2.5	15 minutes

Note: This chart is based on transferring files with a 28,800 bps modem. A 14,400 bps modem or lower will transfer information more slowly than shown in the chart.

If you want to view or play a large file, consider transferring the file during off-peak hours, such as nights and weekends. There is less traffic on the Internet at these times, so the information will transfer more quickly to your computer.

JAVA AND JAVASCRIPT

Java and JavaScript are built-in to Netscape. They allow Web pages to display animation and moving text, play music and much more.

JavaScript is a simplified version of Java.

JAVA AND JAVASCRIPT

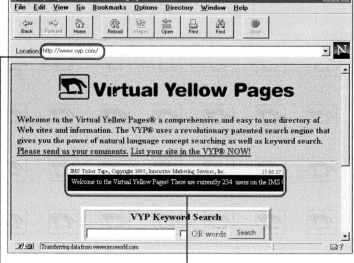

■ In this example, we connect to the page at this address.

Note: To display a Web page, refer to page 18.

■ Java lets you watch animated characters move on your screen while you listen to background music.

■ In this example, we connect to the page at this address.

■ Java lets you view text that blinks or scrolls across your screen.

■ Information, such as stock quotes and weather reports, can update before your eyes.

You can find many examples of Java and JavaScript at the **http://www.gamelan.com** *Web page.*

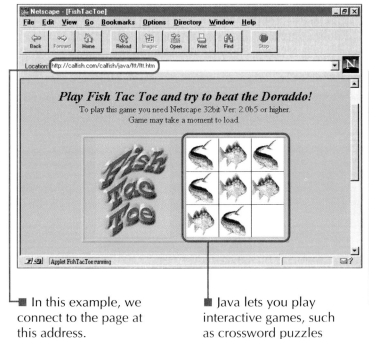

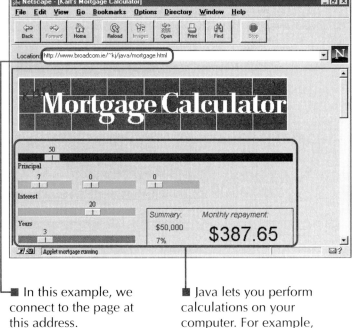

■ In this example, we connect to the page at this address.

■ Java lets you play interactive games, such as crossword puzzles and tic-tac-toe.

■ In this example, we connect to the page at this address.

■ Java lets you perform calculations on your computer. For example, you can calculate your mortgage or car payments.

Netscape comes with a program that lets you listen to sounds on the Web.

Netscape can play sound files with the aif, aifc, aiff, au or snd extension.

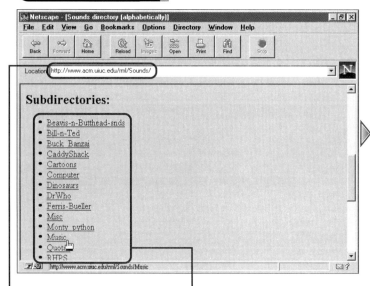

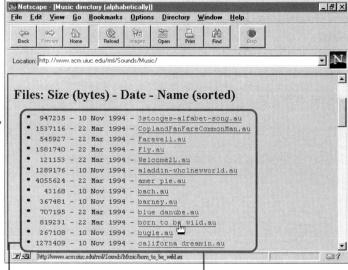

■ In this example, we connect to the page at this address.

Note: To display a Web page, refer to page 18.

1 To display the sounds in one of the available categories, move the mouse ⌐ʰᵐ over the category of interest and then press the left button.

Note: To view the categories, use the scroll bar. For more information, refer to page 23.

■ A list of sounds in the category you selected appears.

2 Move the mouse ⌐ʰᵐ over the sound you want to play and then press the left button.

■ The **Viewing Location** dialog box appears.

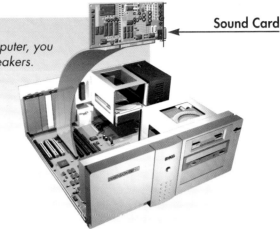

Sound Card

Tip

To hear sound on your computer, you need a sound card and speakers. A sound card is a circuit board that plugs inside a computer to improve the sound quality.

Note: Most Macintosh computers come with sound cards.

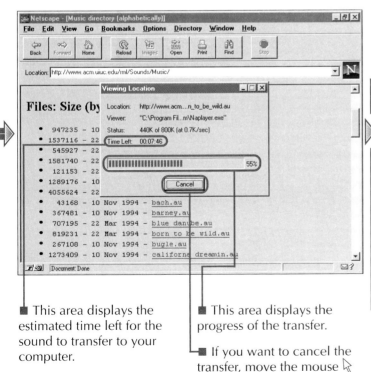

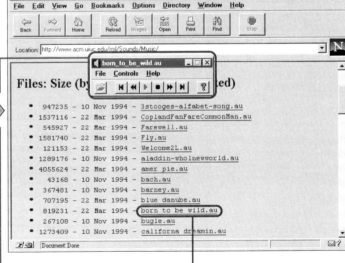

■ This area displays the estimated time left for the sound to transfer to your computer.

■ This area displays the progress of the transfer.

■ If you want to cancel the transfer, move the mouse ⬚ over **Cancel** and then press the left button.

■ When the sound has completely transferred to your computer, this dialog box appears and the sound plays.

■ To replay the sound, move the mouse ⬚ over the item again and then press the left button.

PLUG-INS

INTRODUCTION TO PLUG-INS

Netscape needs special programs, called plug-ins, to display or play certain types of graphics, sound and video on the Web.

A plug-in performs tasks that Netscape cannot perform on its own.

If you want to view or play a graphic, sound or video that Netscape cannot work with, you can download (copy) the appropriate plug-in from the Internet free of charge. After you download a plug-in, the program will work with Netscape to display or play the file.

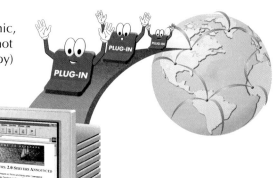

The next pages discuss some plug-ins you may find useful. You can find a list of many plug-ins at the following Web page:

http://home.netscape.com/comprod/products/ navigator/version_2.0/plugins/index.html

ACROBAT AMBER READER

A PDF file is a high-quality document on your screen that looks like a printed document, such as a newspaper or magazine.

PDF files are portable, which means you can view the same PDF file on any type of computer, such as a Macintosh or a PC.

Acrobat Amber Reader can display files with the .pdf extension (example: **resume.pdf**).

Web Pages

■ You can get Acrobat Amber Reader at the following Web page:
http://www.adobe.com/Amber/Download.html

■ You can view a list of Acrobat Amber Reader pages at the following Web page:
http://www.adobe.com/Amber/amexamp.html

■ You can view one full page at a time to see the overall design of a PDF file or zoom in to read the details.

■ You can flip through the pages of a PDF file as you would flip through a printed document.

Crescendo lets you listen to background music to enhance the text and graphics on a Web page.

CRESCENDO

You can try Crescendo for free for a limited time. If you like the program and want to continue using it, you must pay for the program.

Crescendo can play files with the .mid extension (example: **music.mid**).

Web Pages

■ You can get Crescendo at the following Web page:
http://www.liveupdate.com/midi.html

■ You can view a list of Crescendo pages at the following Web page:
http://www.liveupdate.com/sod.html

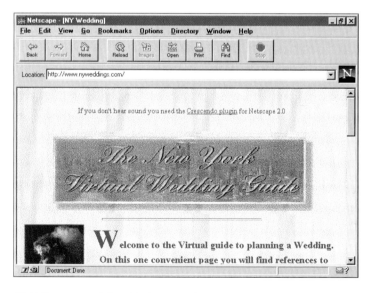

■ When you visit a Web page that uses Crescendo, the music begins to play almost immediately.

Live3D lets you view three-dimensional worlds and images on the Web.

LIVE3D

Live3D lets you use your mouse or keyboard to walk or fly around virtual cities and objects. You can look at objects from the top, front, back or side.

Live3D can display files with the .wrl extension (example: **cafe.wrl**).

Web Pages

■ You can get Live3D at the following Web page:
http://home.netscape.com/comprod/products/navigator/live3d/download_live3d.html

■ You can view a list of Live3D pages at the following Web page:
http://home.netscape.com/comprod/products/navigator/live3d/cool_worlds.html

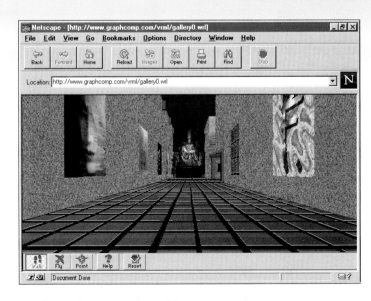

■ Three-dimensional worlds are created using a language called Virtual Reality Modeling Language (VRML).

PLUG-INS

You can use QuickTime to view videos on the Web.

QuickTime lets you play video, music and animation on any type of computer, such as a Macintosh or a PC.

QuickTime can play files with the .mov extension (example: **preview.mov**).

Web Pages

■ You can get QuickTime at the following Web page:
http://quicktime.apple.com

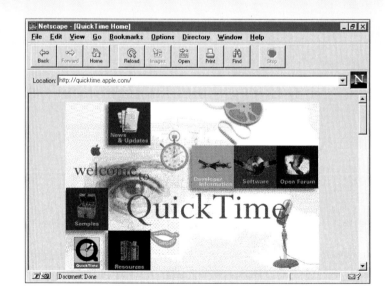

> RealAudio lets you listen to sound files without having to wait.

REALAUDIO

You can use RealAudio to listen to live sounds, such as radio programs, on your computer.

Other programs that play sound transfer the entire sound file to your computer before you hear any sound. RealAudio plays the sound while the file is transferring.

RealAudio can play files with the .ra or .ram extension (example: **hiphop.ra**).

Web Pages

■ You can get RealAudio at the following Web page:
http://www.realaudio.com/products/player2.0.html

■ You can view a list of RealAudio pages at the following Web page:
http://www.realaudio.com/raguide.cgi

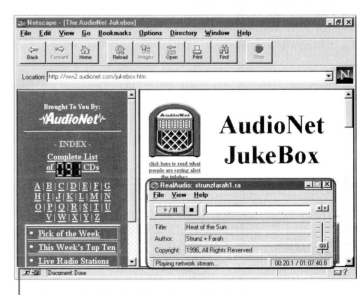

■ When a RealAudio file plays, this window appears. You can adjust the volume or stop playing the file at any time.

PLUG-INS

Shockwave for Director lets you view interactive presentations on the Web.

SHOCKWAVE FOR DIRECTOR

Shockwave for Director lets you display exciting combinations of animation, video, sound and special effects on your screen.

Shockwave for Director can play files with the .dcr extension (example: **logo.dcr**).

Web Pages

■ You can get Shockwave for Director at the following Web page:
http://www.macromedia.com/Tools/Shockwave/sdc/Plugin/index.html

■ You can view a list of Shockwave for Director pages at the following Web page:
http://www.macromedia.com/Gallery/index.html

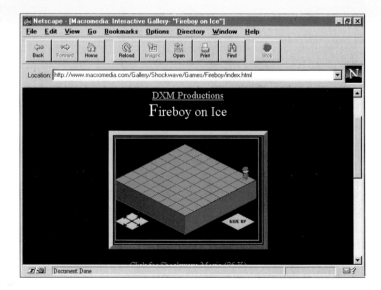

■ You can find games that use Shockwave for Director on the Web.

■ Companies use Shockwave for Director to display multimedia presentations and company logos on the Web.

VDOLIVE

Other programs that play video transfer the entire video file to your computer before you can view the video. VDOLive plays the video while the file is transferring.

VDOLive can play files with the .vdo extension (example: **demo.vdo**).

Web Pages

■ You can get VDOLive at the following Web page:
http://www.vdolive.com/download

■ You can view a list of VDOLive pages at the following Web page:
http://www.vdolive.com/watch

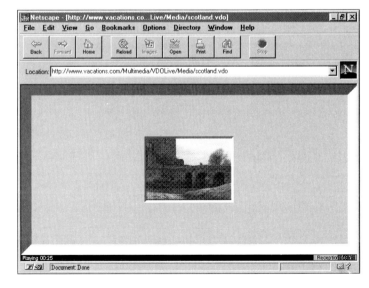

■ Companies use VDOLive to give product demonstrations on the Web.

■ You can use VDOLive to view movie previews or personal ads on the Web.

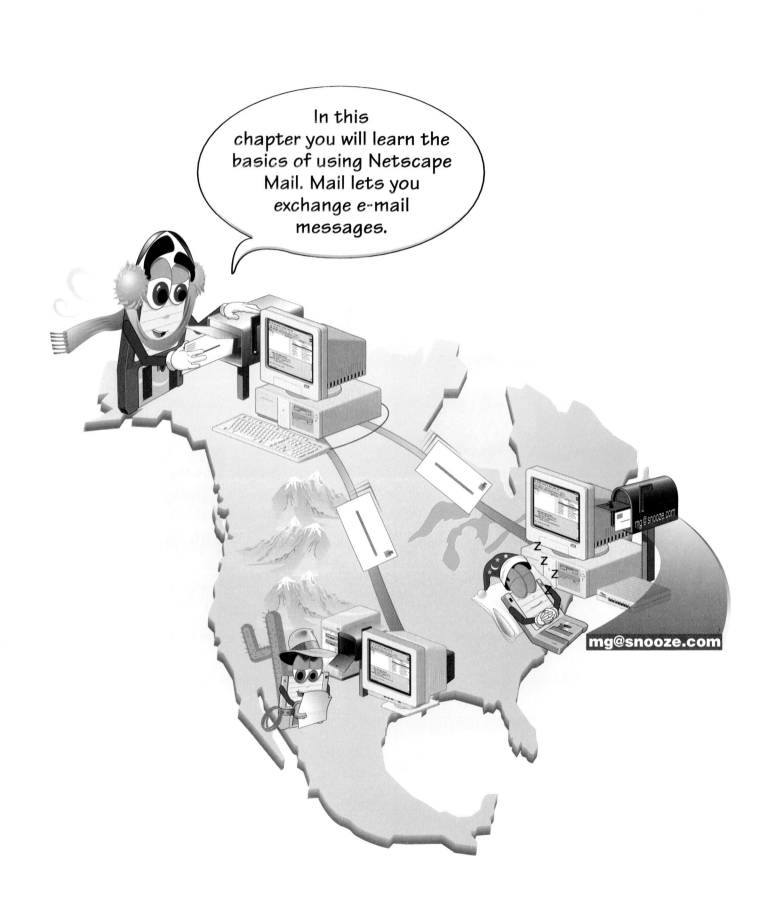

E-MAIL BASICS

Introduction to E-Mail

Start and Exit Netscape Mail

Set Up Mail

Get New Messages

Change Size of Viewing Areas

Read a Message

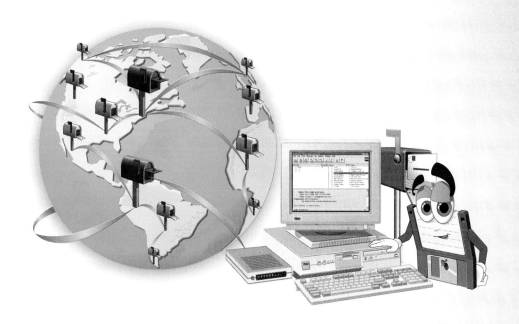

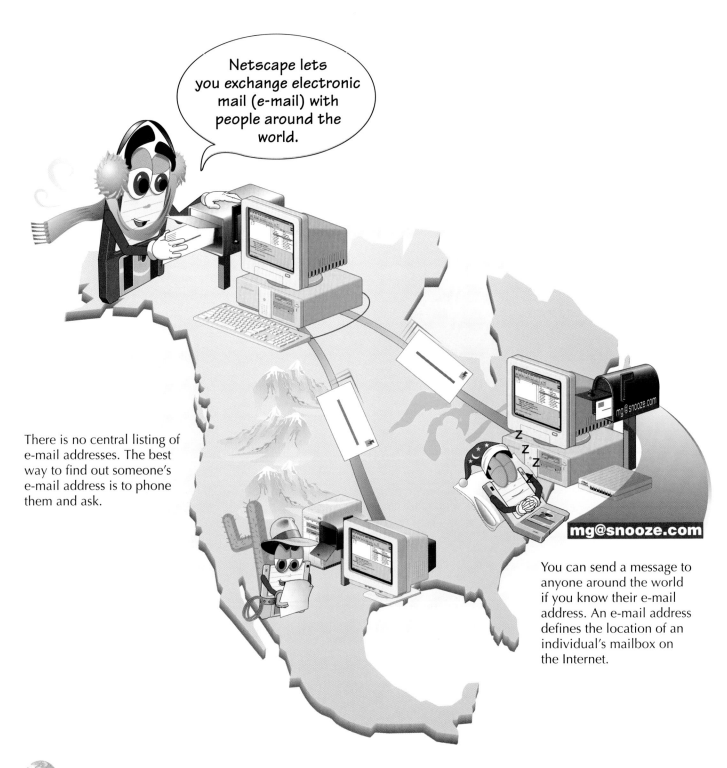

Netscape lets you exchange electronic mail (e-mail) with people around the world.

There is no central listing of e-mail addresses. The best way to find out someone's e-mail address is to phone them and ask.

mg@snooze.com

You can send a message to anyone around the world if you know their e-mail address. An e-mail address defines the location of an individual's mailbox on the Internet.

An e-mail address consists of two parts, separated by the @ (at) symbol. An e-mail address cannot contain spaces.

jsmith@sales.abc.com

USER NAME
The name of the person's account. This can be a real name or a nickname.

DOMAIN NAME
The location of the person's account. Periods (.) separate the various parts of the domain name.

The last few characters in an e-mail address usually indicate the type of organization and/or country the person belongs to. Examples are listed below.

Country

au	Australia
ca	Canada
it	Italy
jp	Japan
us	United States

Organization

com	commercial	mil	military
edu	education	net	network
gov	government	org	organization (often non-profit)

INTRODUCTION TO E-MAIL

COMMON E-MAIL TERMS

SMILEYS

You can use special characters, called smileys or emoticons, to express emotions in messages. These characters resemble human faces if you turn them sideways.

Gesture	Characters
Cry	:'-(
Smile	:-)
Laugh	:-D
Frown	:-(
Surprise	:-0
Wink	;-)
Santa Claus	*<|:-)

Book of Smileys

Gesture	Characters		Gesture	Characters
Cry	:'-(		Wink	;-)
Smile	:-)		Santa Claus	*<	:-)
Laugh	:-D			
Frown	:-(			
Surprise	:-O			

ABBREVIATIONS

Abbreviations are commonly used in messages to save time typing.

Abbreviation	Meaning	Abbreviation	Meaning
BTW	by the way	L8R	later
FAQ	frequently asked questions	LOL	laughing out loud
FOAF	friend of a friend	MOTAS	member of the appropriate sex
FWIW	for what it's worth	MOTOS	member of the opposite sex
FYI	for your information	MOTSS	member of the same sex
IMHO	in my humble opinion	ROTFL	rolling on the floor laughing
IMO	in my opinion	SO	significant other
IOW	in other words	WRT	with respect to

FLAME

A flame is an angry or insulting message directed at one person.

A flame war is an argument that continues for a while. Avoid starting or participating in flame wars.

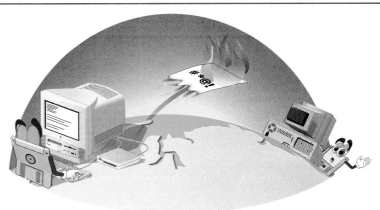

SHOUTING

A MESSAGE WRITTEN IN CAPITAL LETTERS IS ANNOYING AND HARD TO READ. THIS IS CALLED SHOUTING. Always use upper and lower case letters when typing messages.

BOUNCED MESSAGE

A bounced message is a message that returns to you because it cannot reach its destination. A message usually bounces because of typing mistakes in the e-mail address. Before sending a message, double-check the e-mail address.

START AND EXIT NETSCAPE MAIL

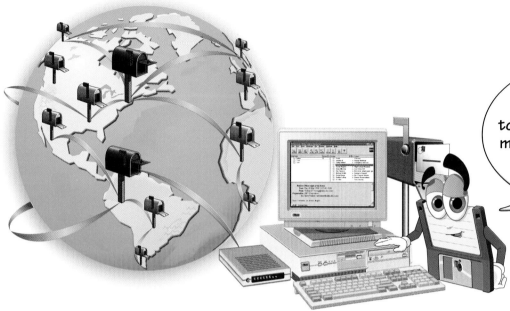

You can use Netscape Mail to exchange electronic messages with people around the world.

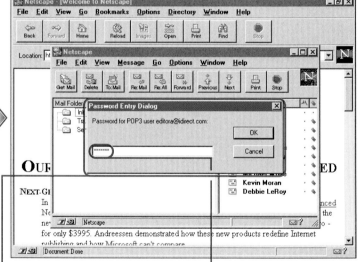

1 Move the mouse ⇖ over this symbol (⊠?) and then press the left button.

■ The Mail window appears.

■ The **Password Entry Dialog** box also appears, asking for your password.

2 Type your password and then press **Enter** on your keyboard.

Note: A symbol (x) appears for each character you type.

Tip

This dialog box appears if you need to set up Mail on your computer.

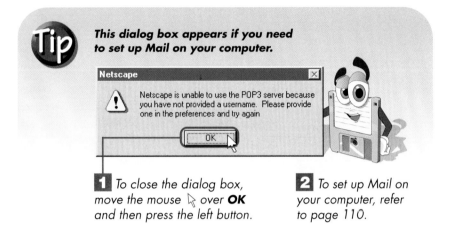

1 To close the dialog box, move the mouse ⃰ over **OK** and then press the left button.

2 To set up Mail on your computer, refer to page 110.

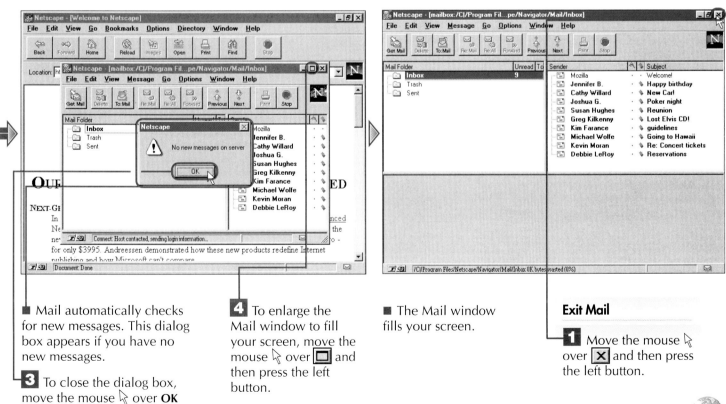

■ Mail automatically checks for new messages. This dialog box appears if you have no new messages.

3 To close the dialog box, move the mouse ⃰ over **OK** and then press the left button.

4 To enlarge the Mail window to fill your screen, move the mouse ⃰ over 🔲 and then press the left button.

■ The Mail window fills your screen.

Exit Mail

1 Move the mouse ⃰ over ✕ and then press the left button.

Before you can use Mail, you must provide information about yourself.

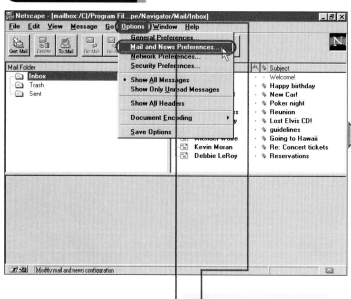

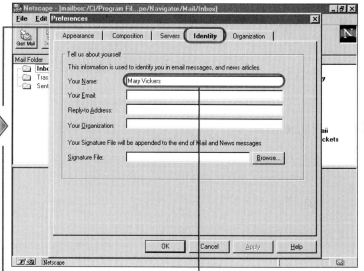

You only need to set up Mail on your computer once.

1 Move the mouse ↖ over **Options** and then press the left button.

2 Move the mouse ↖ over **Mail and News Preferences** and then press the left button.

■ The **Preferences** dialog box appears.

3 Move the mouse ↖ over the **Identity** tab and then press the left button.

4 Move the mouse I over this area and then press the left button. Type your name and then press **Tab** on your keyboard.

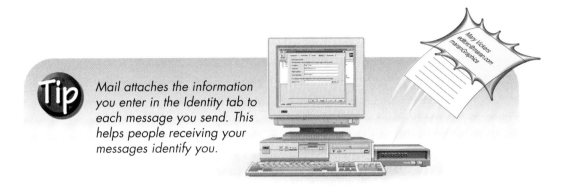

Tip

Mail attaches the information you enter in the Identity tab to each message you send. This helps people receiving your messages identify you.

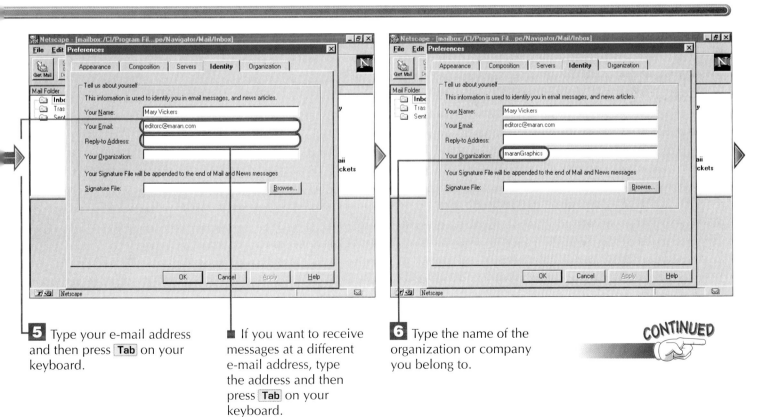

5 Type your e-mail address and then press **Tab** on your keyboard.

■ If you want to receive messages at a different e-mail address, type the address and then press **Tab** on your keyboard.

6 Type the name of the organization or company you belong to.

CONTINUED

When setting up Mail, you must provide information about the computer that sends and receives your messages.

SET UP MAIL (CONTINUED)

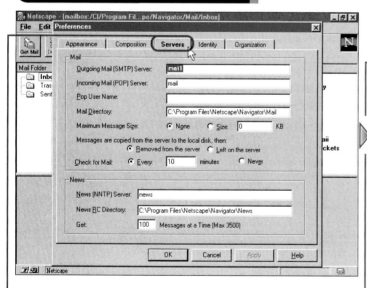

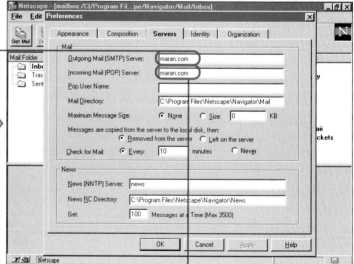

7 Move the mouse ⍉ over the **Servers** tab and then press the left button.

8 Type the address of the computer that sends your messages and then press **Tab** on your keyboard.

9 Type the address of the computer that receives your messages and then press **Tab** on your keyboard.

*Note: For more information, refer to the **Tip** on page 113.*

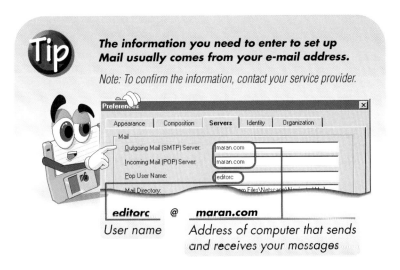

Tip

The information you need to enter to set up Mail usually comes from your e-mail address.

Note: To confirm the information, contact your service provider.

editorc @ maran.com

User name   Address of computer that sends and receives your messages

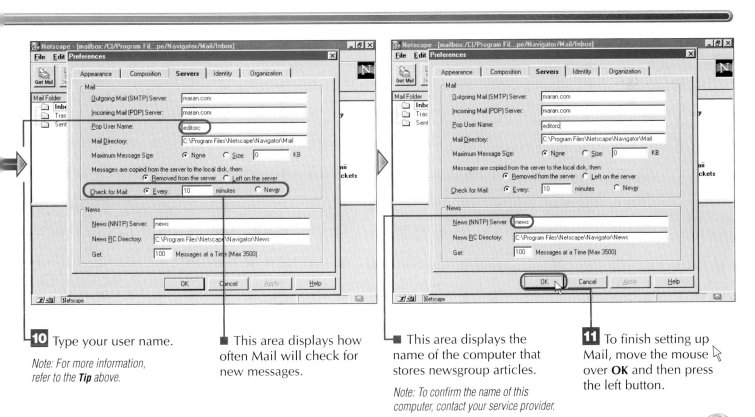

10 Type your user name.

Note: For more information, refer to the **Tip** above.

■ This area displays how often Mail will check for new messages.

■ This area displays the name of the computer that stores newsgroup articles.

Note: To confirm the name of this computer, contact your service provider.

11 To finish setting up Mail, move the mouse over **OK** and then press the left button.

Mail checks for new messages every ten minutes. When you have new messages, you can easily display them on your screen.

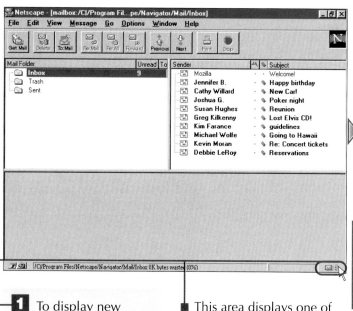

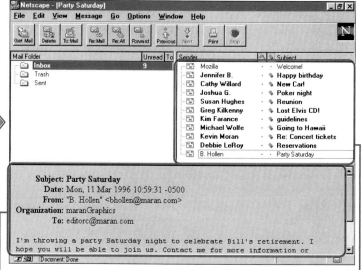

1 To display new messages on your screen, move the mouse ⟍ over this symbol (📧) and then press the left button.

■ This area displays one of three symbols:

📧 You have new messages.

📧 You have no new messages.

📧 Mail cannot check for messages because you are not connected to the Internet or you have not started Mail.

■ This area displays the first new message.

■ This area displays a list of all your messages. Messages you have not read display a diamond (◆) and appear in **bold** type.

CHANGE SIZE OF VIEWING AREAS

Mail displays information in three areas on your screen. You can easily change the size of these areas.

CHANGE SIZE OF VIEWING AREAS

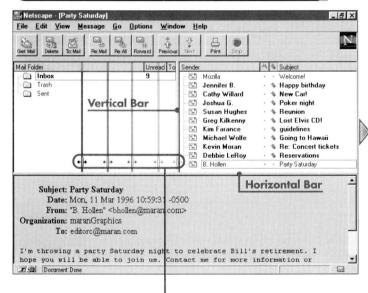

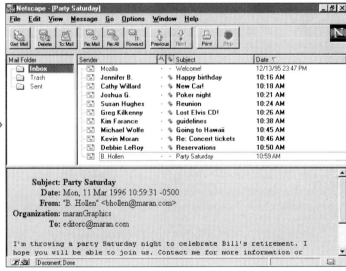

■ You can move the horizontal or vertical bar to change the size of the viewing areas.

1 Move the mouse ⬚ over a bar (⬚ changes to ↔ or ⇕).

2 Press and hold down the left button as you move the bar to a new location. Then release the button.

■ The size of the viewing areas change.

You can easily view the contents of your messages.

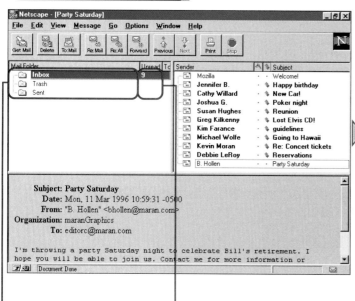

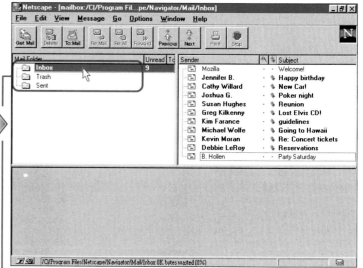

■ This area displays the folders that store your messages.

*Note: The **Trash** folder does not appear on your screen until you delete a message. To delete a message, refer to page 140.*

■ This area displays the number of messages you have not read in each folder.

*Note: If you have read all the messages in a folder, the **Unread** area is empty.*

1 Move the mouse over the folder that contains the messages you want to view and then press the left button.

Mail stores your messages in three folders.

Inbox
Stores messages
sent to you.

Trash
Stores messages
you have deleted.

Sent
Stores messages
you have sent.

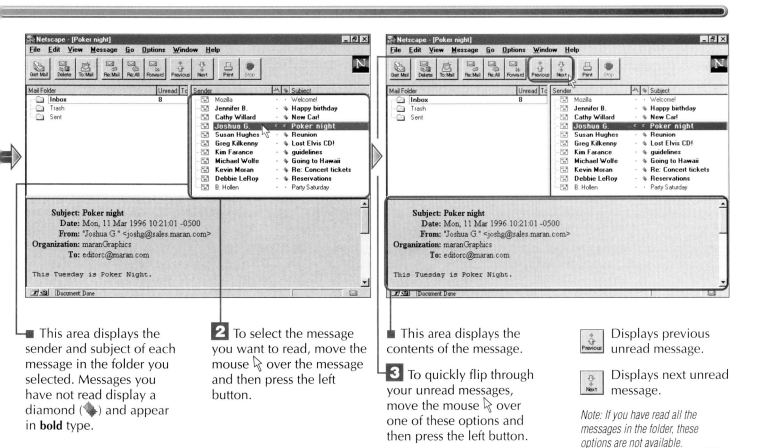

■ This area displays the sender and subject of each message in the folder you selected. Messages you have not read display a diamond (◆) and appear in **bold** type.

2 To select the message you want to read, move the mouse over the message and then press the left button.

■ This area displays the contents of the message.

3 To quickly flip through your unread messages, move the mouse over one of these options and then press the left button.

Displays previous unread message.

Displays next unread message.

Note: If you have read all the messages in the folder, these options are not available.

117

CHAPTER 8

SEND AND RECEIVE MESSAGES

 Add a Name to the Address Book

 Send a Message

 Attach a File to a Message

 View an Attached File

 Reply to a Message

 Forward a Message

 Create a Signature File

Mail provides an address book where you can store the e-mail addresses of people you frequently send messages to.

ADD A NAME TO THE ADDRESS BOOK

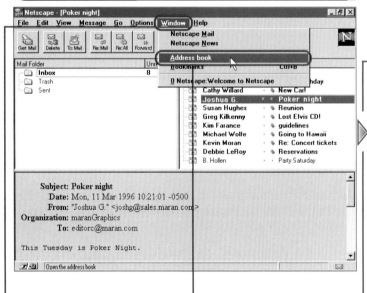

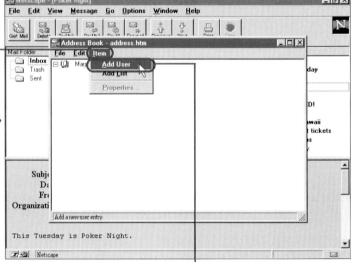

■ To start Mail, refer to page 108.

1 Move the mouse ⟨ over **Window** and then press the left button.

2 Move the mouse ⟨ over **Address book** and then press the left button.

■ The **Address Book** window appears.

3 To add a person to the address book, move the mouse ⟨ over **Item** and then press the left button.

4 Move the mouse ⟨ over **Add User** and then press the left button.

■ The **Address Book** dialog box appears.

Tip

When sending a message, you can use a name stored in the address book. This saves you from having to type the same addresses over and over again.

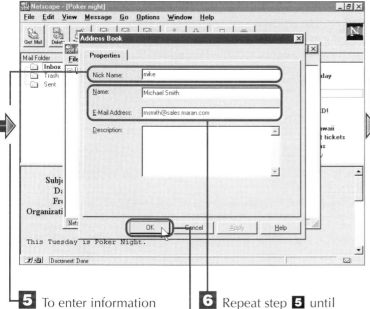

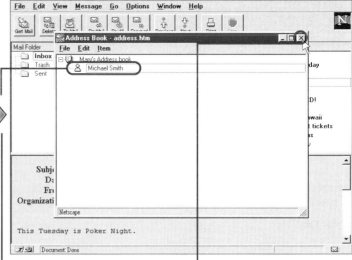

5 To enter information about the person you want to add to the address book, type the information that corresponds to the first item. Then press **Tab** on your keyboard.

Note: A nickname can be a name or any humorous or descriptive word. Nicknames can only contain lower case letters and no spaces.

6 Repeat step **5** until you have entered all the information.

7 Move the mouse ⌀ over **OK** and then press the left button.

■ Mail adds the name to the address book.

■ To remove a name from the address book, move the mouse ⌀ over the name and then press the left button. Then press **Delete** on your keyboard.

8 To close the **Address Book** window, move the mouse ⌀ over ⊠ and then press the left button.

Note: To send a message using a name from the address book, refer to page 124.

ADD A NAME TO THE ADDRESS BOOK

When you receive a message from a colleague or friend, you can quickly add their name to the address book.

QUICKLY ADD A NAME TO THE ADDRESS BOOK

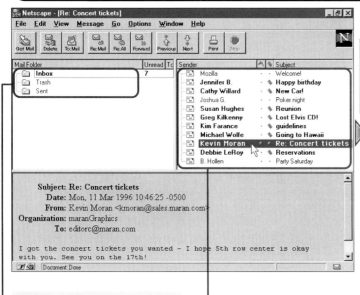

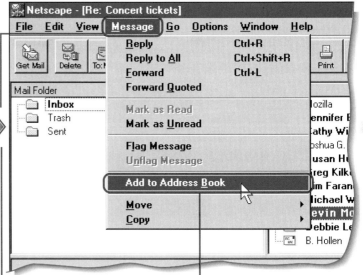

1 To display the message sent by the person you want to add to the address book, move the mouse ⬚ over the folder that contains the message and then press the left button.

2 Move the mouse ⬚ over the message and then press the left button.

3 Move the mouse ⬚ over **Message** and then press the left button.

4 Move the mouse ⬚ over **Add to Address Book** and then press the left button.

■ The **Address Book** dialog box appears.

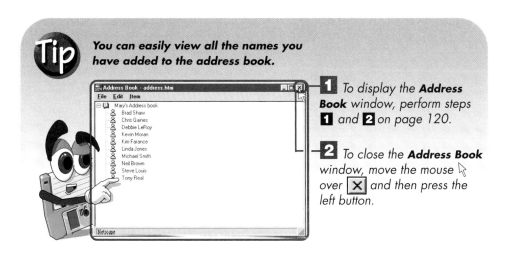

You can easily view all the names you
have added to the address book.

1 To display the **Address Book** window, perform steps **1** and **2** on page 120.

2 To close the **Address Book** window, move the mouse over ☒ and then press the left button.

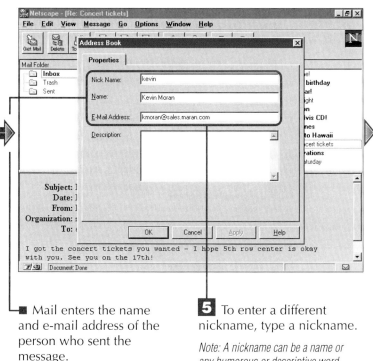

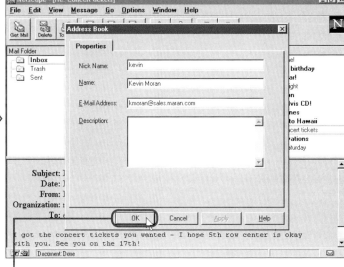

■ Mail enters the name and e-mail address of the person who sent the message.

Note: If Mail finds a nickname, it will also appear in this area.

5 To enter a different nickname, type a nickname.

Note: A nickname can be a name or any humorous or descriptive word. Nicknames can only contain lower case letters and no spaces.

6 Move the mouse over **OK** and then press the left button.

■ Mail adds the name to the address book.

Note: To send a message using a name from the address book, refer to page 124.

You can send a message to exchange ideas or request information.

To practice sending a message, send a message to yourself.

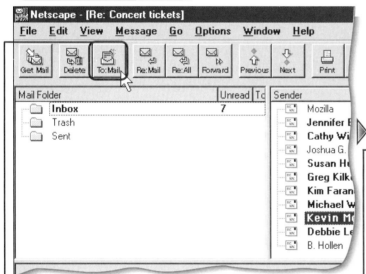

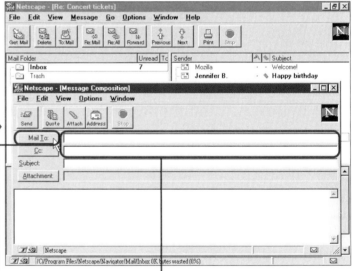

1 Move the mouse over 🖳 and then press the left button.

■ The **Message Composition** window appears.

2 To select the name of each person you want to receive the message from your address book, move the mouse over **Mail To:** and then press the left button.

■ You can also type the nickname (**mike**) or the e-mail address (**msmith@sales.maran.com**) of each person you want to receive the message in these areas. To complete the message, perform steps **8** to **10** starting on page 126.

*Note: When typing more than one name or address in an area, separate each item with a comma (example: **mike**, **chris**).*

A carbon copy (**Cc**) is an exact copy of a message. You can send a carbon copy of your message to a person who is not directly involved, but would be interested in the message.

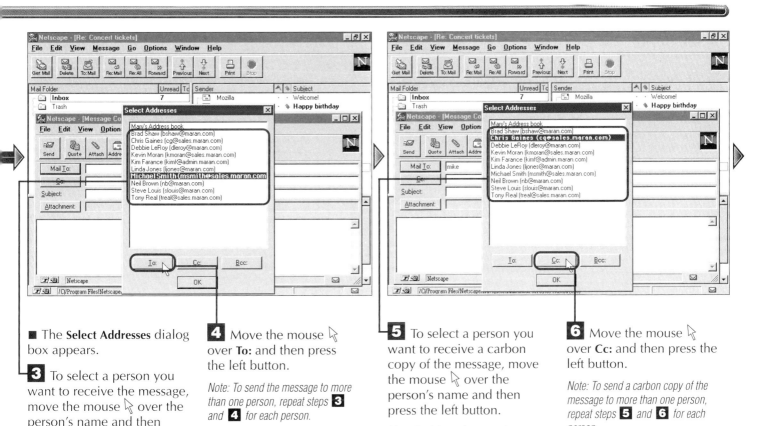

■ The **Select Addresses** dialog box appears.

3 To select a person you want to receive the message, move the mouse ⌖ over the person's name and then press the left button.

4 Move the mouse ⌖ over **To:** and then press the left button.

*Note: To send the message to more than one person, repeat steps **3** and **4** for each person.*

5 To select a person you want to receive a carbon copy of the message, move the mouse ⌖ over the person's name and then press the left button.

*Note: For information on carbon copies, refer to the **Tip** above.*

6 Move the mouse ⌖ over **Cc:** and then press the left button.

*Note: To send a carbon copy of the message to more than one person, repeat steps **5** and **6** for each person.*

CONTINUED

When typing a message, make sure the message is clear, concise and contains no spelling or grammar errors.

SEND A MESSAGE (CONTINUED)

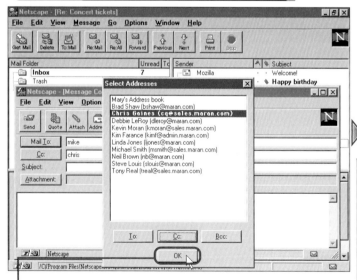

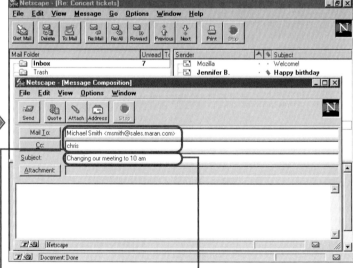

7 When you have finished selecting the people you want to receive the message, move the mouse ⬚ over **OK** and then press the left button.

■ These areas display the names of the people who will receive the message.

8 To enter a subject for the message, move the mouse I over this area and then press the left button. Then type the subject of the message.

Note: Make sure the subject clearly identifies the contents of your message.

Tip

When you send a message, do not assume the person receiving the message will read it right away. Some people may not regularly check their messages.

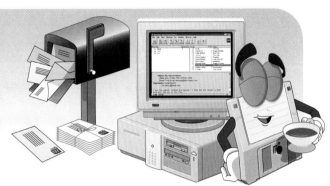

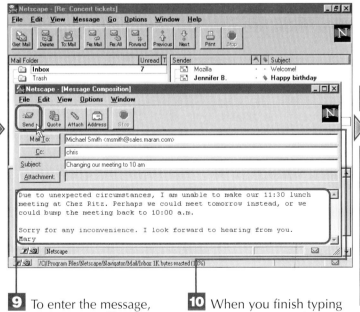

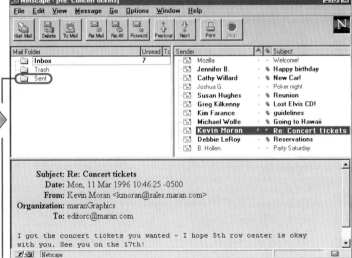

9 To enter the message, move the mouse I over this area and then press the left button. Then type the message.

Note: To attach a file to the message, refer to page 128.

10 When you finish typing the message, move the mouse ⌖ over 🖃 and then press the left button.

■ Mail sends the message and stores a copy of the message in the **Sent** folder.

You can attach a file to a message you are sending. This is useful when you want to include additional information with the message.

Dear Bill,

Along with this letter I have included the film. The film is included to help you better understand what is in hand here. As you will see, this project will require many long hours and a lot of manpower.

Keep in touch, and call if you have questions.

John Keeran

ATTACH A FILE TO A MESSAGE

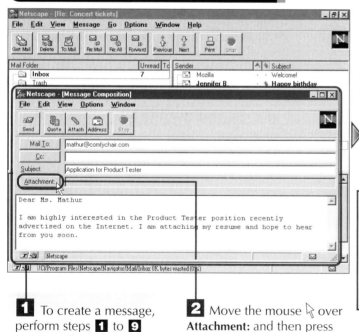

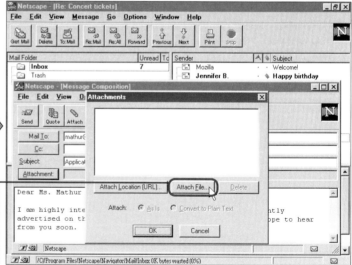

1 To create a message, perform steps **1** to **9** starting on page 124.

2 Move the mouse ▷ over **Attachment:** and then press the left button.

■ The **Attachments** dialog box appears.

3 To attach a file, move the mouse ▷ over **Attach File** and then press the left button.

■ The **Enter file to attach** dialog box appears.

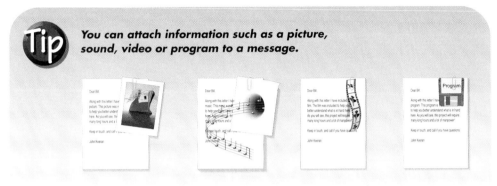

Tip

You can attach information such as a picture, sound, video or program to a message.

The computer receiving the message must have the necessary software to display the picture, hear the sound, view the video or run the program.

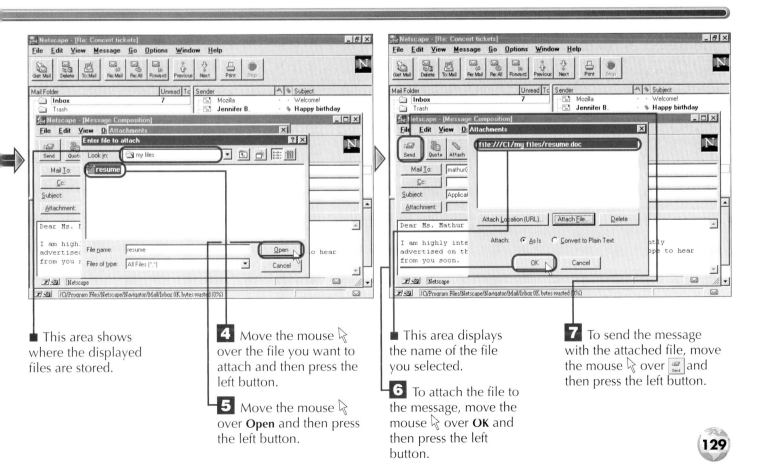

■ This area shows where the displayed files are stored.

4 Move the mouse ⍩ over the file you want to attach and then press the left button.

5 Move the mouse ⍩ over **Open** and then press the left button.

■ This area displays the name of the file you selected.

6 To attach the file to the message, move the mouse ⍩ over **OK** and then press the left button.

7 To send the message with the attached file, move the mouse ⍩ over [icon] and then press the left button.

A message you receive may have an attached file. You can easily save and then view the file.

ATTACHED FILE

ABC CORPORATION

<u>EMPLOYEE GUIDELINES</u>
1996

VIEW AN ATTACHED FILE

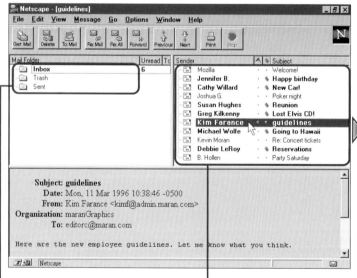

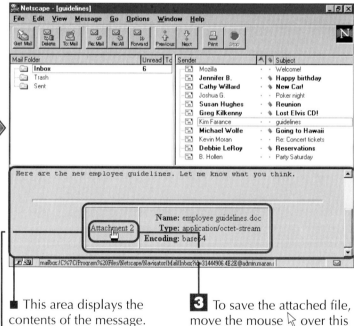

1 Move the mouse ⇧ over the folder that contains the message you want to view and then press the left button.

2 Move the mouse ⇧ over the message and then press the left button.

■ This area displays the contents of the message.

■ If a message contains an attached file, this information appears at the bottom of the message.

3 To save the attached file, move the mouse ⇧ over this area (⇧ changes to ᵐ) and then press the left button.

■ The **Save As** dialog box appears.

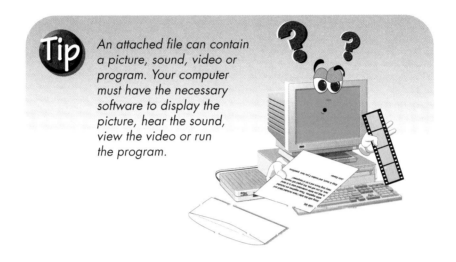

Tip

An attached file can contain a picture, sound, video or program. Your computer must have the necessary software to display the picture, hear the sound, view the video or run the program.

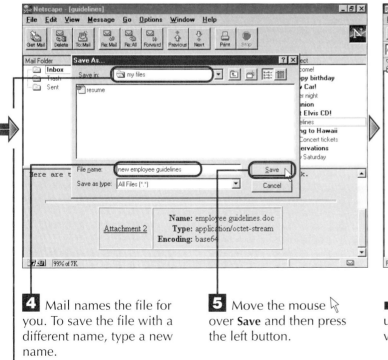

4 Mail names the file for you. To save the file with a different name, type a new name.

■ This area displays where Mail will save the file.

5 Move the mouse ⤢ over **Save** and then press the left button.

■ You can now open the file using a program that lets you view the file.

Note: In this example, we use a word processing program to display a document.

You can reply to a message to answer a question, express an opinion or supply additional information.

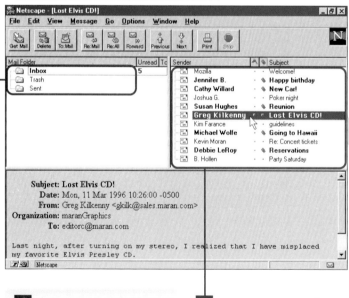

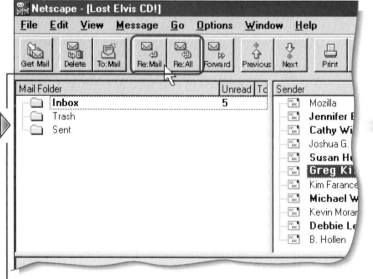

1 Move the mouse ⃞ over the folder that contains the message you want to reply to and then press the left button.

2 Move the mouse ⃞ over the message and then press the left button.

3 Move the mouse ⃞ over a reply option and then press the left button.

Re:Mail Replies to author.

Re:All Replies to author and everyone who received the original message.

Tip

Exchanging electronic mail can save you money on long distance calls to colleagues, friends and family. The next time you are about to pick up the telephone, consider sending an e-mail message instead.

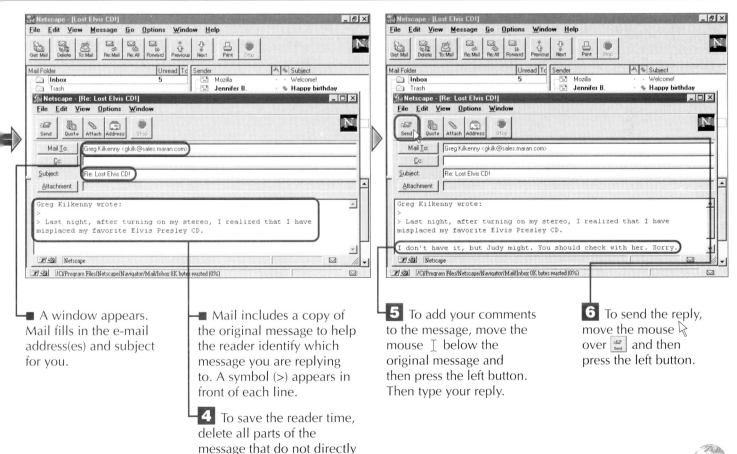

■ A window appears. Mail fills in the e-mail address(es) and subject for you.

■ Mail includes a copy of the original message to help the reader identify which message you are replying to. A symbol (>) appears in front of each line.

4 To save the reader time, delete all parts of the message that do not directly relate to your reply.

5 To add your comments to the message, move the mouse I below the original message and then press the left button. Then type your reply.

6 To send the reply, move the mouse over [Send] and then press the left button.

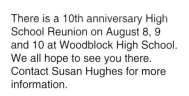

There is a 10th anniversary High School Reunion on August 8, 9 and 10 at Woodblock High School. We all hope to see you there. Contact Susan Hughes for more information.

Rick, I thought you might be interested in the reunion. Unfortunately, I will be out of town.

After reading a message, you can add comments and then send the message to a friend or colleague.

FORWARD A MESSAGE

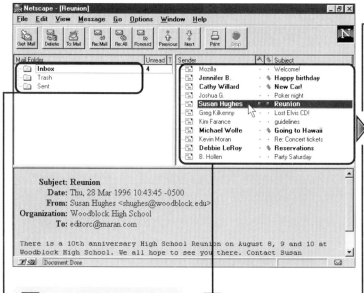

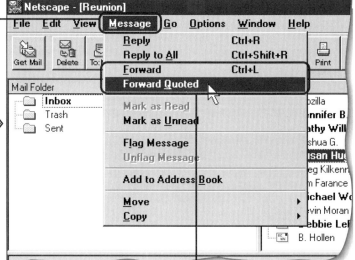

1 Move the mouse ⬉ over the folder that contains the message you want to forward and then press the left button.

2 Move the mouse ⬉ over the message and then press the left button.

3 Move the mouse ⬉ over **Message** and then press the left button.

4 Move the mouse ⬉ over the way you want to forward the message and then press the left button.

Note: For information on the forward options, refer to the top of page 135.

There are two ways you can forward a message.

Forward

Displays the message you are forwarding and your comments in separate sections. This option is ideal if the message you are forwarding has an attached file.

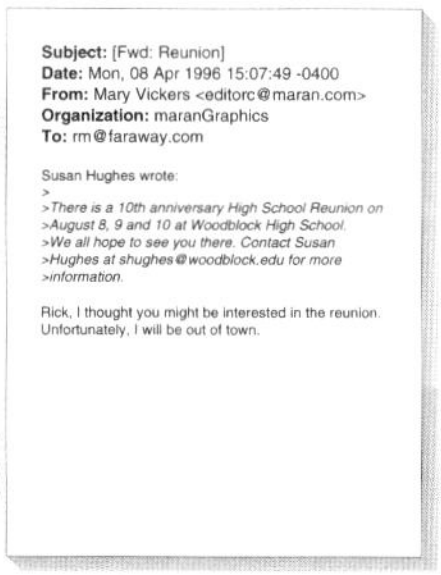

Forward Quoted

Displays your comments with the message you are forwarding. This option is ideal if the message you are forwarding contains text you want to edit.

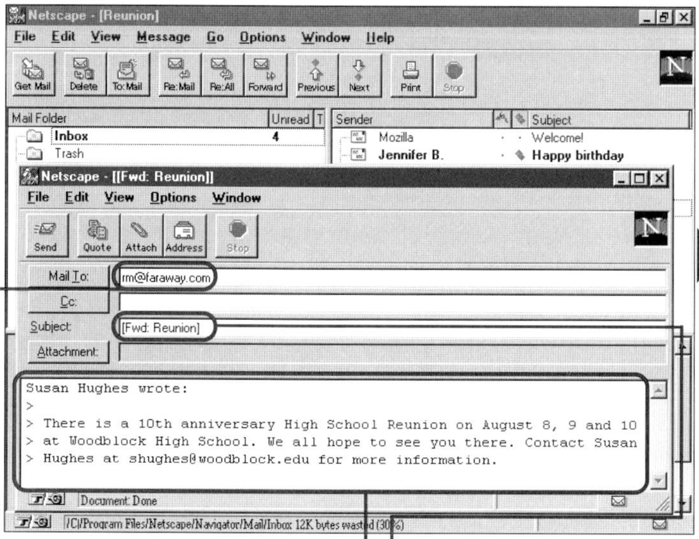

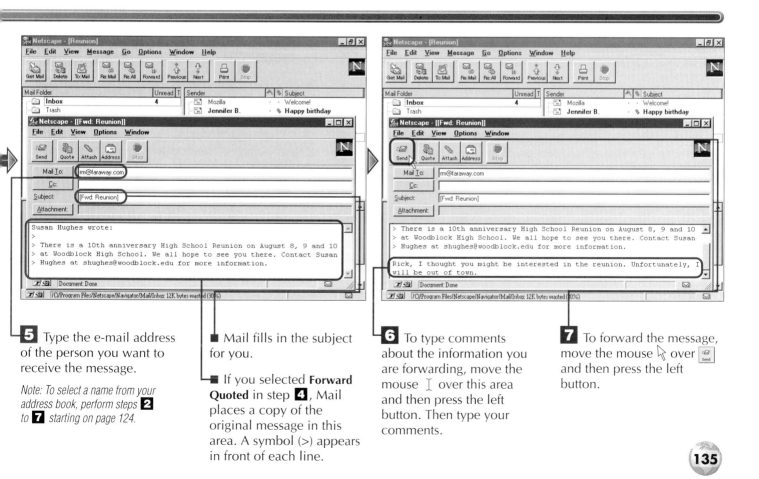

5 Type the e-mail address of the person you want to receive the message.

*Note: To select a name from your address book, perform steps **2** to **7** starting on page 124.*

■ Mail fills in the subject for you.

■ If you selected **Forward Quoted** in step **4**, Mail places a copy of the original message in this area. A symbol (>) appears in front of each line.

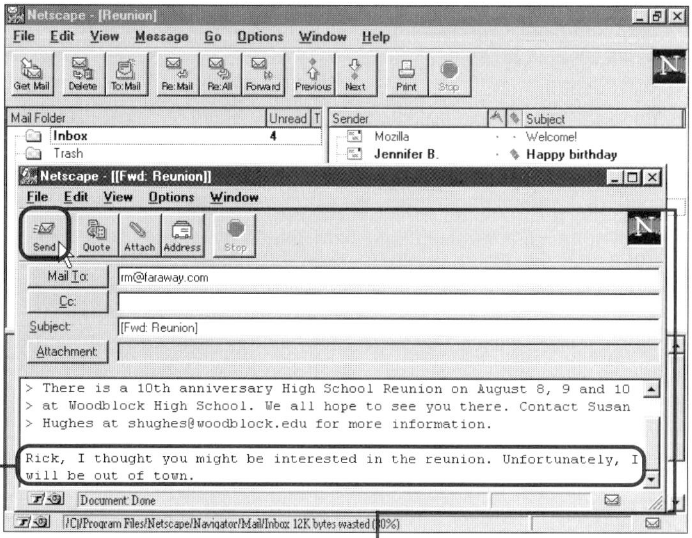

6 To type comments about the information you are forwarding, move the mouse I over this area and then press the left button. Then type your comments.

7 To forward the message, move the mouse over Send and then press the left button.

You can have Mail add information about yourself to the end of every message you send. This prevents you from having to type the same information over and over.

mg@maran.com
spokesperson
handsome, suave, debonair

CREATE A SIGNATURE FILE

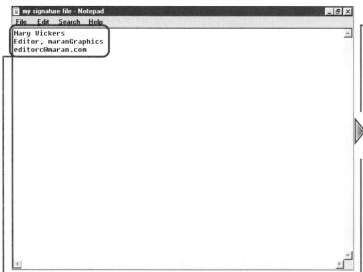

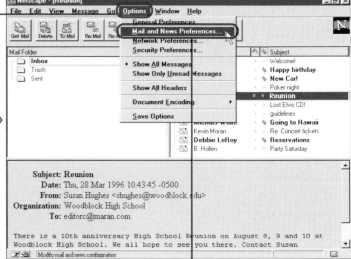

1 In a text editor such as **Notepad**, type and save the information you want to attach to the end of all your messages.

Note: A text editor is a program that only lets you create simple documents without any formatting.

2 In Mail, move the mouse ⟶ over **Options** and then press the left button.

3 Move the mouse ⟶ over **Mail and News Preferences** and then press the left button.

■ The **Preferences** dialog box appears.

A signature file can include information such as your name, e-mail address, occupation or favorite quotation. You can also use plain characters to display simple pictures.

Do not create a signature file that is more than four lines long.

John Smith
Sales Manager
ABC Corporation
jsmith@sales.abc.com

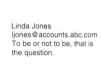

Linda Jones
ljones@accounts.abc.com
To be or not to be, that is
the question.

(_ @ _)
M
_M_
_| |_ Jill Martin

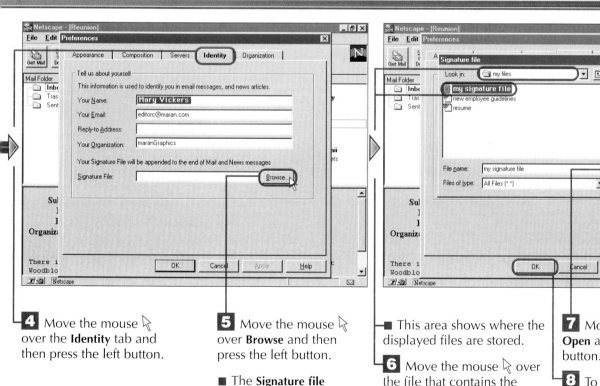

4 Move the mouse ↖ over the **Identity** tab and then press the left button.

5 Move the mouse ↖ over **Browse** and then press the left button.

■ The **Signature file** dialog box appears.

■ This area shows where the displayed files are stored.

6 Move the mouse ↖ over the file that contains the information you want to attach to the end of all your messages and then press the left button.

7 Move the mouse ↖ over **Open** and then press the left button.

8 To confirm the file you selected, move the mouse ↖ over **OK** and then press the left button.

CHAPTER 9

WORK WITH MESSAGES

 Delete a Message

 Preview a Message

 Print a Message

 Mark a Message as Unread

 Flag a Message

 Sort Messages

 Create a New Folder

 Move a Message

 Find a Message

 Find Text in a Message

You can delete a message you no longer need. This prevents your folders from overflowing with messages.

DELETE A MESSAGE

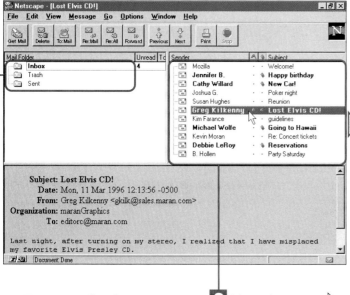

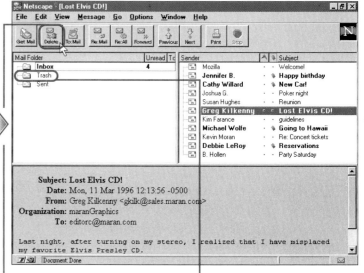

■ To start Mail, refer to page 108.

1 Move the mouse ↳ over the folder containing the message you want to delete and then press the left button.

2 Move the mouse ↳ over the message and then press the left button.

3 To delete the message, move the mouse ↳ over [Delete] and then press the left button.

■ Mail places the message in the **Trash** folder.

*Note: The **Trash** folder does not appear on your screen until you delete a message.*

You can delete all the messages
in the Trash folder to permanently remove
the messages from your computer.

EMPTY TRASH FOLDER

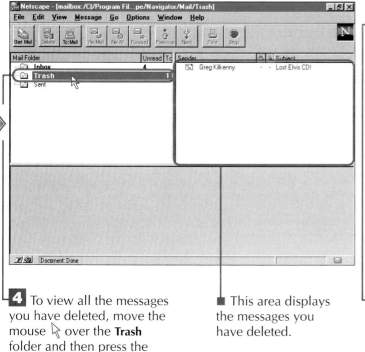

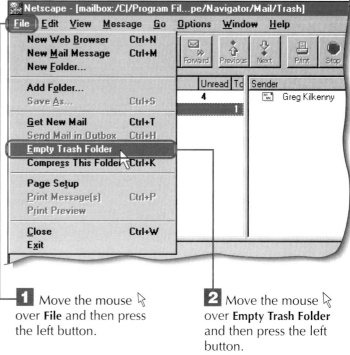

4 To view all the messages
you have deleted, move the
mouse over the **Trash**
folder and then press the
left button.

■ This area displays
the messages you
have deleted.

1 Move the mouse
over **File** and then press
the left button.

2 Move the mouse
over **Empty Trash Folder**
and then press the left
button.

You can see on the screen how an e-mail message will look when printed.

PREVIEW A MESSAGE

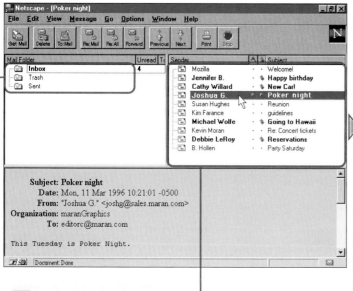

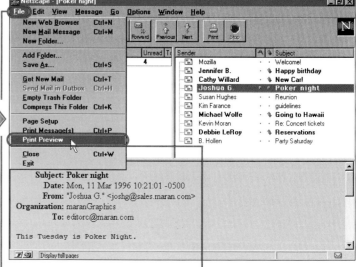

1 Move the mouse ⇖ over the folder containing the message you want to preview and then press the left button.

2 Move the mouse ⇖ over the message and then press the left button.

3 Move the mouse ⇖ over **File** and then press the left button.

4 Move the mouse ⇖ over **Print Preview** and then press the left button.

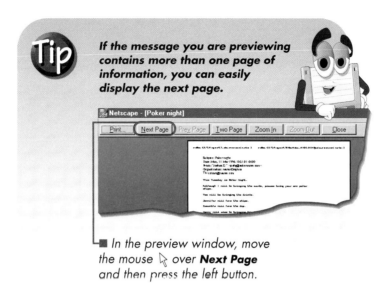

Tip

If the message you are previewing contains more than one page of information, you can easily display the next page.

■ In the preview window, move the mouse ⟍ over **Next Page** and then press the left button.

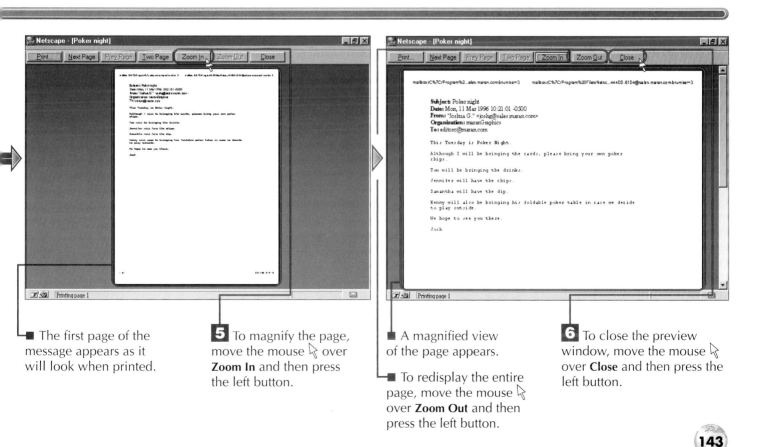

■ The first page of the message appears as it will look when printed.

5 To magnify the page, move the mouse ⟍ over **Zoom In** and then press the left button.

■ A magnified view of the page appears.

■ To redisplay the entire page, move the mouse ⟍ over **Zoom Out** and then press the left button.

6 To close the preview window, move the mouse ⟍ over **Close** and then press the left button.

PRINT A MESSAGE

You can produce a paper copy of a message displayed on your screen.

PRINT A MESSAGE

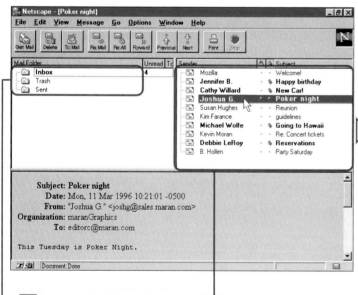

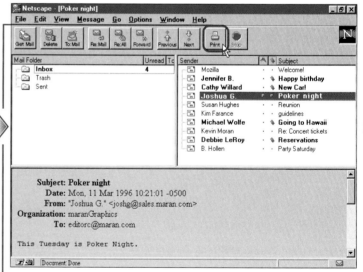

1 Move the mouse ⇱ over the folder containing the message you want to print and then press the left button.

2 Move the mouse ⇱ over the message and then press the left button.

3 Move the mouse ⇱ over 🖶 and then press the left button.

You can use the Print
Preview feature to
see on screen how
a message will look
when printed.

*Note: For more information,
refer to page 142.*

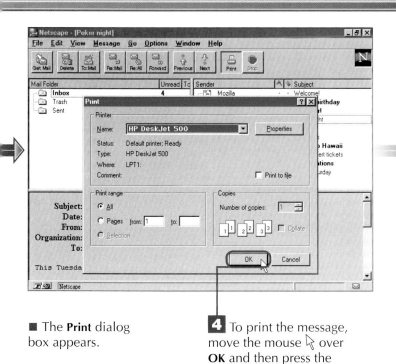

■ The **Print** dialog
box appears.

4 To print the message,
move the mouse ⍩ over
OK and then press the
left button.

■ Mail prints the page number
and the current date and time
on each page.

MARK A MESSAGE AS UNREAD

You can make a message appear as if you have not read the message. This will remind you to read the message again the next time you start Mail.

MARK A MESSAGE AS UNREAD

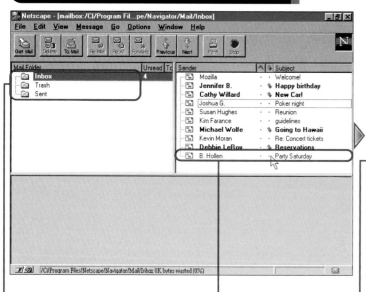

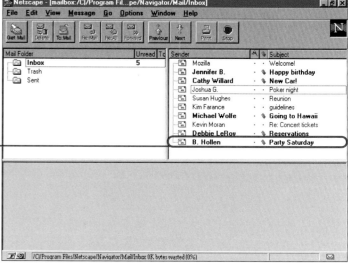

1 Move the mouse ⟨ over the folder containing the message you want to mark as unread and then press the left button.

2 To mark a message as unread, move the mouse ⟨ over the dot (•) closest to the subject of the message and then press the left button.

■ The message displays a diamond (◈) and appears in **bold** type.

146

FLAG A MESSAGE

You can place a flag beside an important message. The message will stand out when you review your messages.

FLAG A MESSAGE

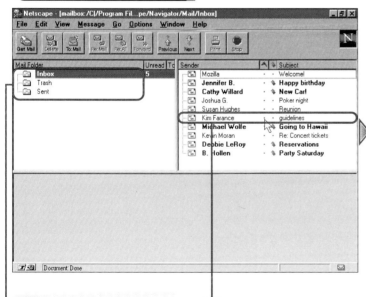

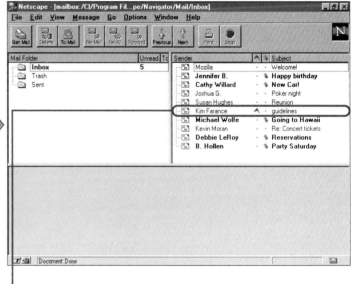

1 Move the mouse ⌖ over the folder containing the message you want to flag and then press the left button.

2 To flag a message, move the mouse ⌖ over the dot (·) closest to the sender of the message and then press the left button.

■ The message displays a flag (🚩).

SORT MESSAGES

You can sort your messages to help you find messages more easily.

SORT MESSAGES

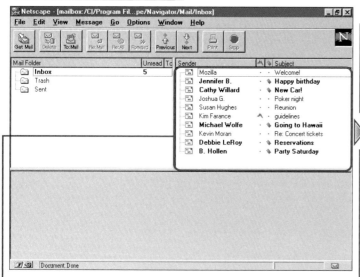

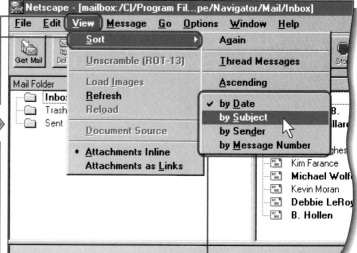

■ Mail automatically sorts your messages by date.

1 To change the way Mail sorts your messages, move the mouse ⬉ over **View** and then press the left button.

2 Move the mouse ⬉ over **Sort**.

3 Move the mouse ⬉ over the way you want to sort the messages and then press the left button.

*Note: For more information, refer to the **Tip** on page 149.*

Tip

You can sort your messages in four different ways.

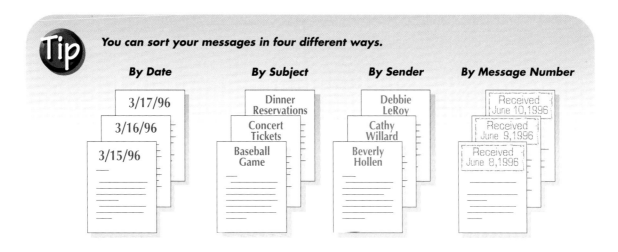

By Date	By Subject	By Sender	By Message Number
3/17/96	Dinner Reservations	Debbie LeRoy	Received June 10,1996
3/16/96	Concert Tickets	Cathy Willard	Received June 9,1996
3/15/96	Baseball Game	Beverly Hollen	Received June 8,1996

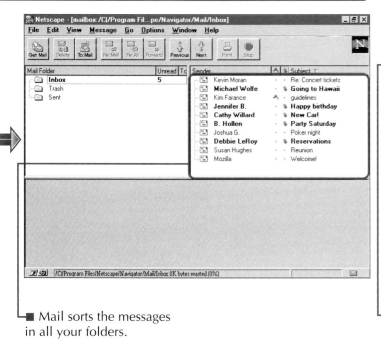

■ Mail sorts the messages in all your folders.

QUICKLY SORT MESSAGES

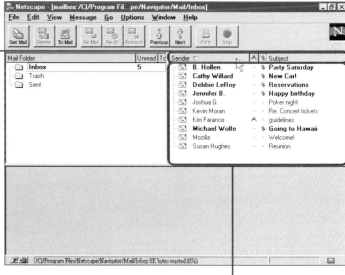

1 To quickly sort your messages, move the mouse over the heading you want to sort by and then press the left button.

Note: If you cannot see the heading you want to sort by, you can enlarge the viewing area. To do so, refer to page 115.

■ Mail sorts the messages in all your folders.

CREATE A NEW FOLDER

You can create a new folder to help you better organize your messages.

MESSAGE
MESSAGE
MESSAGE

NEW FOLDER

CREATE A NEW FOLDER

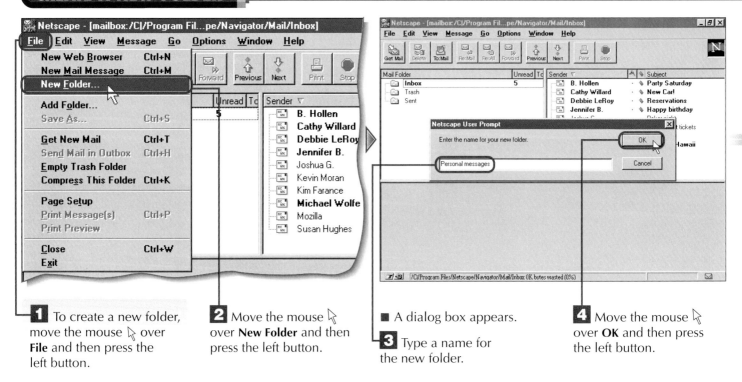

1 To create a new folder, move the mouse ⩥ over **File** and then press the left button.

2 Move the mouse ⩥ over **New Folder** and then press the left button.

■ A dialog box appears.

3 Type a name for the new folder.

4 Move the mouse ⩥ over **OK** and then press the left button.

You can delete a folder
you no longer need.

DELETE A FOLDER

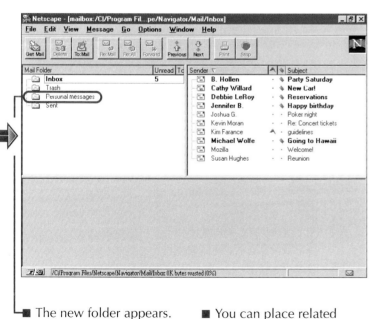

■ The new folder appears.

■ You can place related
messages in the new folder.
This helps you keep your
messages organized.

*Note: To move a message to
a folder, refer to page 152.*

■ You cannot delete a
folder containing messages.
To delete messages in a
folder, refer to page 140.

1 Move the mouse
over the folder you want
to delete and then press
the left button.

2 Press **Delete** on
your keyboard.

MOVE A MESSAGE

You can reorganize your messages by placing them in different folders.

MOVE A MESSAGE

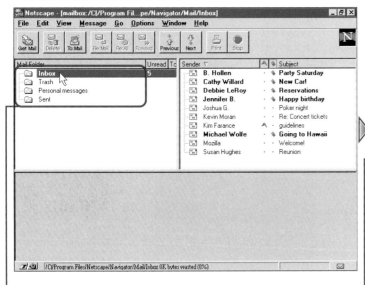

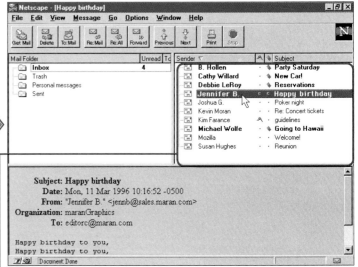

1 Move the mouse ⌖ over the folder containing the message you want to move and then press the left button.

2 To select the message you want to move, position the mouse ⌖ over the message and then press the left button.

Tip

E-mail is much faster than old-fashioned mail, called "snail mail." An e-mail message can travel around the world in seconds.

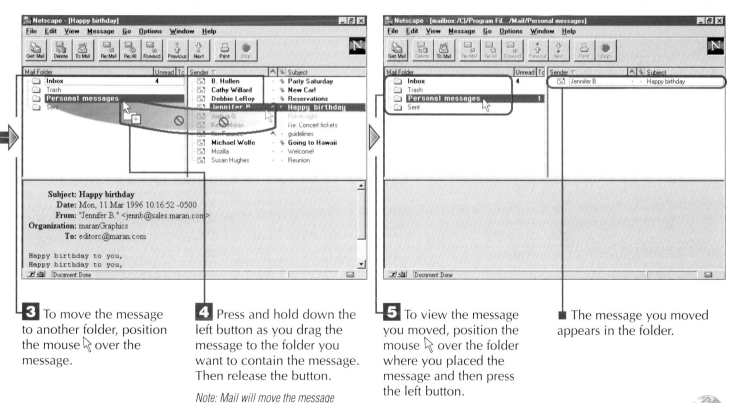

3 To move the message to another folder, position the mouse ⏚ over the message.

4 Press and hold down the left button as you drag the message to the folder you want to contain the message. Then release the button.

Note: Mail will move the message into the folder you highlight.

5 To view the message you moved, position the mouse ⏚ over the folder where you placed the message and then press the left button.

■ The message you moved appears in the folder.

FIND A MESSAGE

You can quickly locate a message by searching the subject of each message in a folder. This is useful when a folder contains a lot of messages.

FIND A MESSAGE

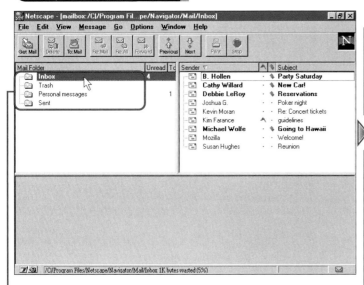

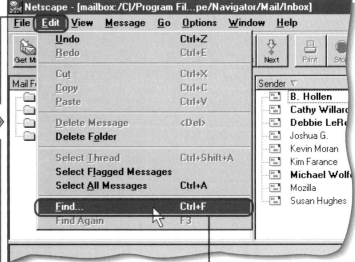

1 Move the mouse ⬚ over the folder containing the message you want to find and then press the left button.

2 Move the mouse ⬚ over **Edit** and then press the left button.

3 Move the mouse ⬚ over **Find** and then press the left button.

■ The **Find** dialog box appears.

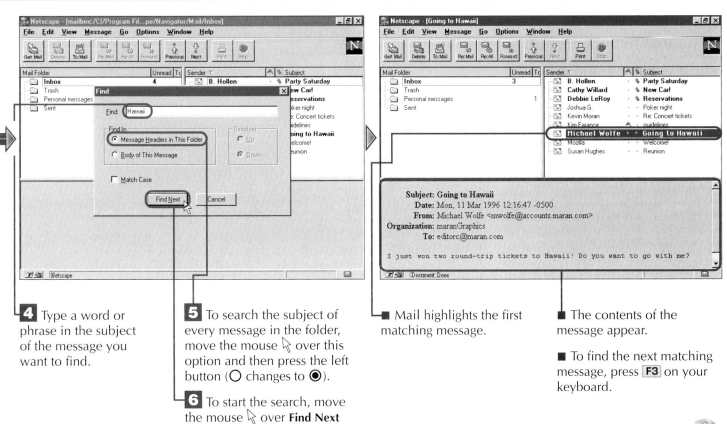

4 Type a word or phrase in the subject of the message you want to find.

5 To search the subject of every message in the folder, move the mouse ⌖ over this option and then press the left button (○ changes to ◉).

6 To start the search, move the mouse ⌖ over **Find Next** and then press the left button.

■ Mail highlights the first matching message.

■ The contents of the message appear.

■ To find the next matching message, press **F3** on your keyboard.

Tip

If you spend a lot of time searching for messages, divide your messages into separate folders. Folders help organize your messages just as folders help organize files in a filing cabinet.

Note: To create a folder, refer to page 150.

Personal | Current Projects | Budget Information

You can search for a word or phrase in a message. This lets you quickly locate areas of interest in the message.

FIND TEXT IN A MESSAGE

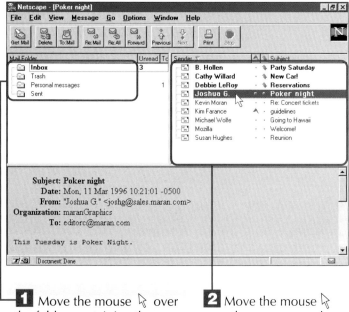

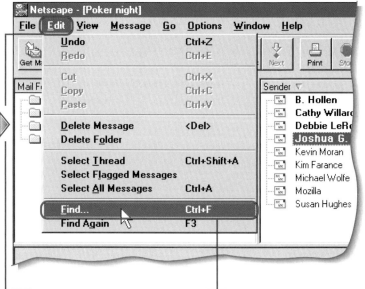

1 Move the mouse ⬚ over the folder containing the message you want to search and then press the left button.

2 Move the mouse ⬚ over the message and then press the left button.

3 Move the mouse ⬚ over **Edit** and then press the left button.

4 Move the mouse ⬚ over **Find** and then press the left button.

■ The **Find** dialog box appears.

Tip

This dialog box appears when the search is complete.

Netscape

Search String Not Found!

OK

■ To close the dialog box, move the mouse ⌖ over **OK** and then press the left button.

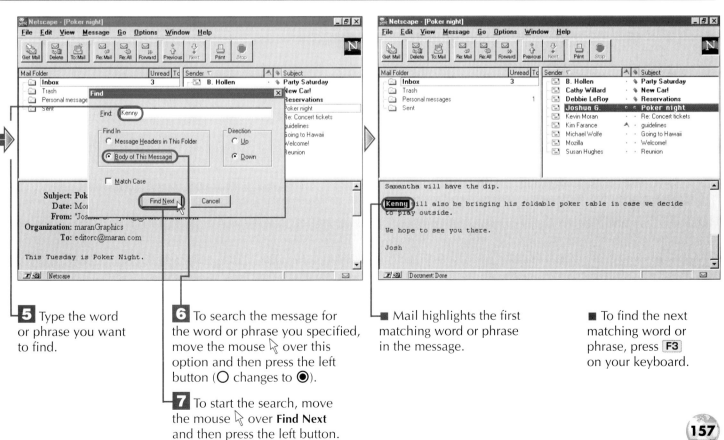

5 Type the word or phrase you want to find.

6 To search the message for the word or phrase you specified, move the mouse ⌖ over this option and then press the left button (○ changes to ◉).

7 To start the search, move the mouse ⌖ over **Find Next** and then press the left button.

■ Mail highlights the first matching word or phrase in the message.

■ To find the next matching word or phrase, press **F3** on your keyboard.

CHAPTER 10

NEWSGROUP BASICS

Introduction to Newsgroups

Start and Exit Netscape News

Subscribe to a Newsgroup

Display All Newsgroups

Change Display of Newsgroups

There are thousands of newsgroups on every subject imaginable. Each newsgroup discusses a particular topic, such as basketball, chemistry or UFOs.

Newsgroup name

The name of a newsgroup describes the type of information discussed in the newsgroup. A name consists of two or more words, separated by periods.

rec . sport.basketball.pro

■ The first word describes the main topic area (example: **rec** for **rec**reation).

■ Each of the following words narrows the topic area.

Article

An article is a message that an individual posts (sends) to a newsgroup.

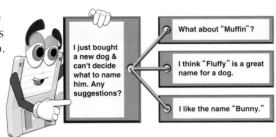

Thread

A thread is an article and all replies to the article. An example of a thread is an initial question and all the responses from other readers.

Carefully choose your words

An article that you post to a newsgroup can be read by tens of thousands of people around the world.

■ The subject of an article is the first item people read. Make sure your subject heading clearly identifies the contents of your article. For example, the subject heading "Read this now" or "For your information" is not very informative.

■ Make sure your article will not be misinterpreted. For example, not all readers will realize a statement is meant to be sarcastic.

■ Make sure your article is clear, concise and contains no spelling or grammar errors.

FAQ

The FAQ (Frequently Asked Questions) is a document that contains a list of questions and answers that regularly appear in a newsgroup. The FAQ prevents new readers from asking the same questions over and over again. Make sure you read the FAQ before posting any articles to a newsgroup.

*Note: The **news.answers** newsgroup provides FAQs for a wide variety of newsgroups.*

INTRODUCTION TO NEWSGROUPS

THE MAIN NEWSGROUP CATEGORIES

alt
General interest discussions that are often bizarre and outrageous. Newsgroups in this category include:

> alt.animals.dolphins
> alt.fan.actors
> alt.music.alternative

biz
Business discussions that are usually more commercial in nature than those of other newsgroups. Advertising is allowed and lists of job openings are available. Newsgroups in this category include:

biz.books.technical
biz.jobs.offered
biz.marketplace.computers.discussion

comp
Discussions of computer hardware, software and computer science. Newsgroups in this category include:

> comp.lang.pascal.borland
> comp.security.misc
> comp.sys.laptops

misc
Discussions of miscellaneous topics that may overlap topics discussed in other categories. Newsgroups in this category include:

> misc.consumers.house
> misc.entrepreneurs
> misc.taxes

news

Discussions about newsgroups in general. Topics range from information about the newsgroup network to advice on how to use it. Newsgroups in this category include:

news.admin.misc
news.announce.newusers
news.newusers.questions

rec

Discussions of recreational activities and hobbies. Newsgroups in this category include:

rec.arts.movies.reviews
rec.food.recipes
rec.sport.football.pro

sci

Discussions about science, including research, applied science and the social sciences. Newsgroups in this category include:

sci.agriculture
sci.energy
sci.virtual-worlds

soc

Discussions of social issues, including world cultures and political issues. Newsgroups in this category include:

soc.college
soc.culture.caribbean
soc.politics

talk

Debates and long discussions, often about controversial subjects. Newsgroups in this category include:

talk.environment
talk.philosophy.misc
talk.rumors

START AND EXIT NETSCAPE NEWS

Netscape News lets you access thousands of discussion groups, called newsgroups.

START NETSCAPE NEWS

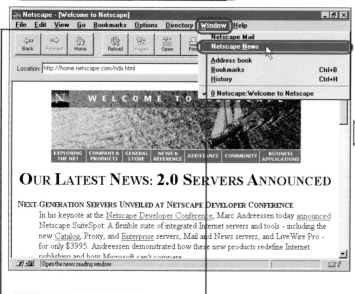

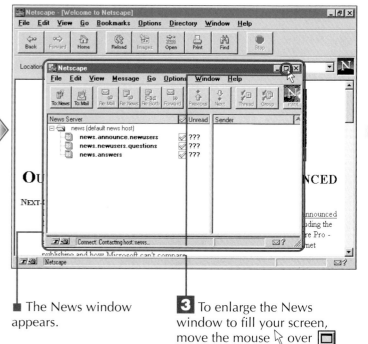

1 Move the mouse ⬉ over **Window** and then press the left button.

2 Move the mouse ⬉ over **Netscape News** and then press the left button.

■ The News window appears.

3 To enlarge the News window to fill your screen, move the mouse ⬉ over ⬜ and then press the left button.

164

IMPORTANT

Before using News, you must give Netscape information about yourself and the computer that sends and receives your messages. To do so, perform the steps starting on page 110.

EXIT NETSCAPE NEWS

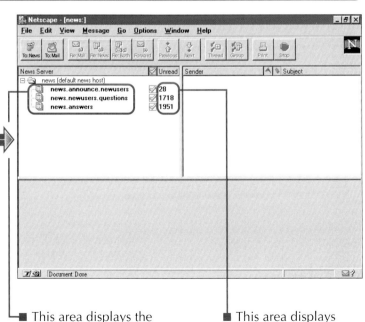

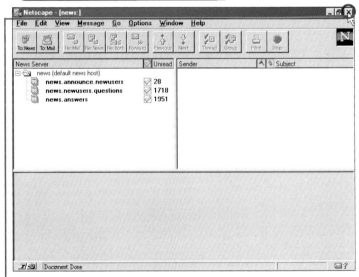

■ This area displays the newsgroups you are currently subscribed to. Netscape automatically subscribes you to three newsgroups that are helpful to beginners.

Note: To subscribe to other newsgroups, refer to page 166.

■ This area displays the number of articles you have not read in each newsgroup.

1 To exit Netscape News, move the mouse ⌖ over 🗙 and then press the left button.

SUBSCRIBE TO A NEWSGROUP

You can subscribe to a newsgroup you want to read regularly.

• Subscribe •
- alt.censorship
☑ - rec.skiing
- talk.environment

SUBSCRIBE TO A NEWSGROUP

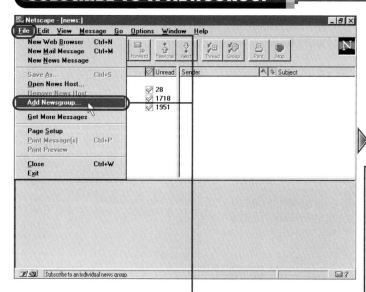

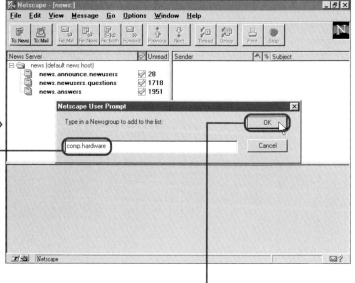

■ If you do not know the name of a newsgroup you want to subscribe to, you can display a list of all the available newsgroups. To do so, refer to page 168.

1 Move the mouse ⇖ over **File** and then press the left button.

2 Move the mouse ⇖ over **Add Newsgroup** and then press the left button.

■ A dialog box appears.

3 Type the name of the newsgroup you want to read on a regular basis.

4 Move the mouse ⇖ over **OK** and then press the left button.

When you no longer want to read a newsgroup on a regular basis, unsubscribe from the newsgroup.

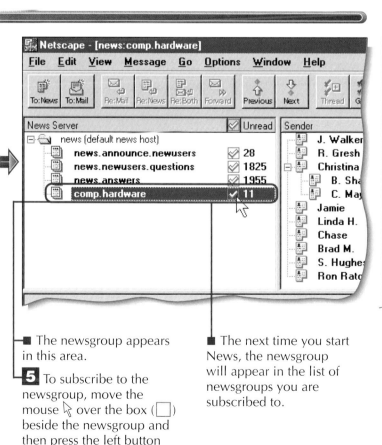

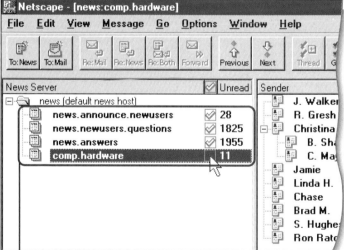

■ The newsgroup appears in this area.

5 To subscribe to the newsgroup, move the mouse ⇘ over the box (☐) beside the newsgroup and then press the left button (☐ changes to ☑).

■ The next time you start News, the newsgroup will appear in the list of newsgroups you are subscribed to.

1 Move the mouse ⇘ over the box (☑) beside the newsgroup and then press the left button (☑ changes to ☐).

■ The next time you start News, the newsgroup will not appear in the list of newsgroups you are subscribed to.

DISPLAY ALL NEWSGROUPS

You can display a list of all the available newsgroups. This helps you find newsgroups of interest.

Newsgroup List

◆ alt.archery
◆ alt.bigfoot
◆ alt.book.reviews
◆ alt.coffee
◆ alt.crime
◆ alt.dreams
◆ alt.guitar

Continued....

DISPLAY ALL NEWSGROUPS

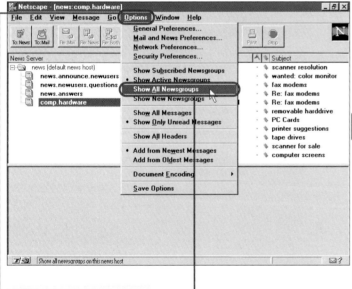

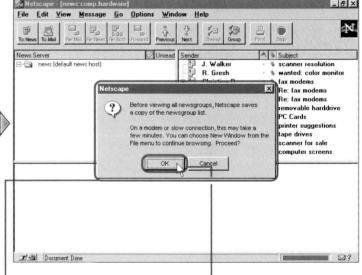

1 Move the mouse ⅄ over **Options** and then press the left button.

2 Move the mouse ⅄ over **Show All Newsgroups** and then press the left button.

■ This dialog box appears the first time you display all newsgroups. The dialog box warns that transferring the newsgroups to your computer may take a few minutes.

3 To transfer the newsgroups, move the mouse ⅄ over **OK** and then press the left button.

■ The newsgroups appear in alphabetical order.

The available newsgroups depend on your service provider. Your list of newsgroups may be different from the list shown below.

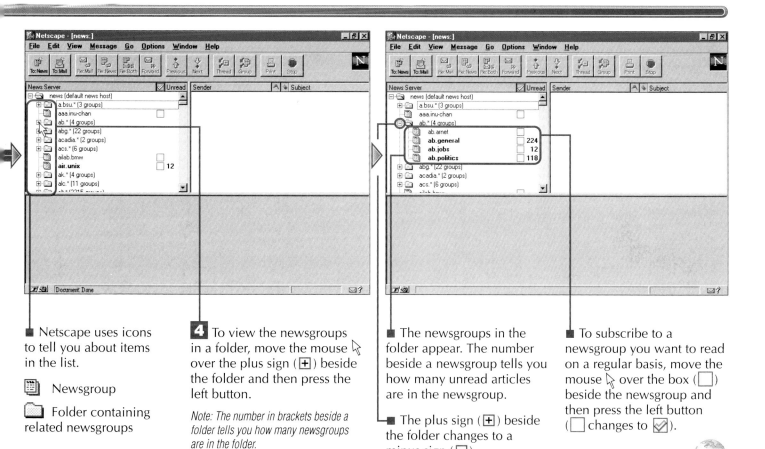

■ Netscape uses icons to tell you about items in the list.

📋 Newsgroup

📁 Folder containing related newsgroups

4 To view the newsgroups in a folder, move the mouse over the plus sign (⊞) beside the folder and then press the left button.

Note: The number in brackets beside a folder tells you how many newsgroups are in the folder.

■ The newsgroups in the folder appear. The number beside a newsgroup tells you how many unread articles are in the newsgroup.

■ The plus sign (⊞) beside the folder changes to a minus sign (⊟).

■ To subscribe to a newsgroup you want to read on a regular basis, move the mouse over the box (☐) beside the newsgroup and then press the left button (☐ changes to ☑).

CHANGE DISPLAY OF NEWSGROUPS

You can specify which newsgroups you want to display on your screen.

Show Subscribed Newsgroups
Displays all the newsgroups you are subscribed to.

Note: To subscribe to a newsgroup, refer to page 166.

CHANGE DISPLAY OF NEWSGROUPS

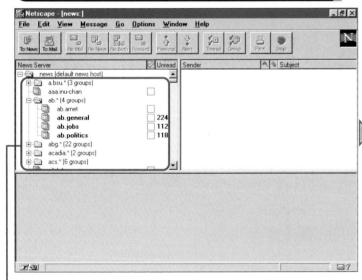

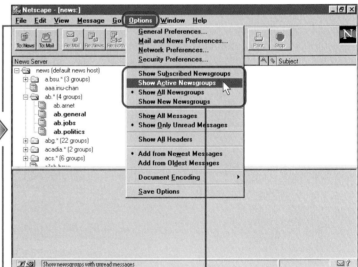

■ This area displays a list of newsgroups.

1 To change which newsgroups appear on your screen, move the mouse ⌖ over **Options** and then press the left button.

2 Move the mouse ⌖ over the newsgroups you want to display and then press the left button.

*Note: If you are selecting **Show All Newsgroups** for the first time, refer to page 168 for more information.*

Show Active Newsgroups
Displays the newsgroups you are subscribed to that contain articles you have not read.

Show All Newsgroups
Displays all the available newsgroups.

Show New Newsgroups
Displays all the newsgroups created since you last started News.

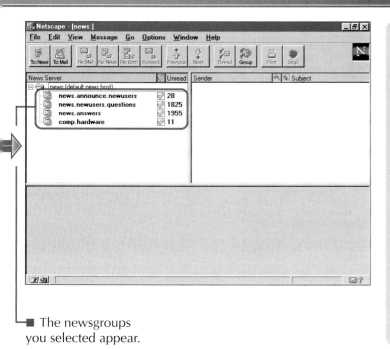

■ The newsgroups you selected appear.

If you selected <u>Show New Newsgroups</u> in step **2**, this dialog box appears telling you how many new newsgroups have been created.

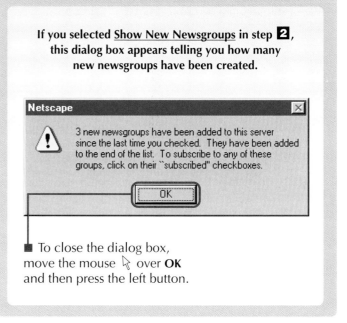

■ To close the dialog box, move the mouse ⤵ over **OK** and then press the left button.

CHAPTER

11

WORK WITH ARTICLES

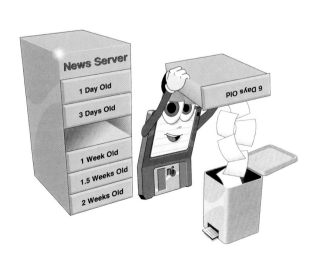

READ AN ARTICLE

You can read articles to learn the opinions and ideas of thousands of people around the world.

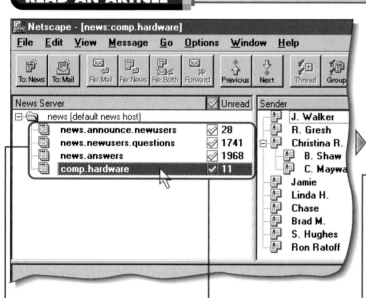

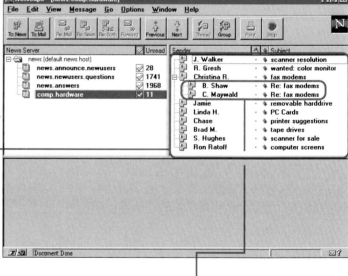

■ To start Netscape News, refer to page 164.

■ This area displays newsgroups and the number of articles you have not read in each newsgroup.

1 Move the mouse over the newsgroup that contains the article you want to read and then press the left button.

■ This area displays the author and subject of each article in the newsgroup you selected.

■ Replies to articles start with **Re:** and are indented.

People are constantly sending new articles to newsgroups to express opinions and answer questions. To keep up-to-date, check for new articles every day.

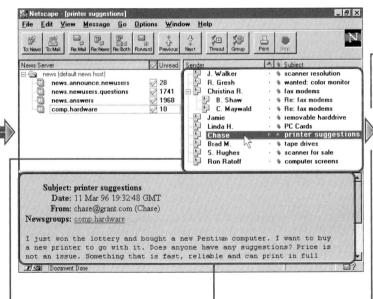

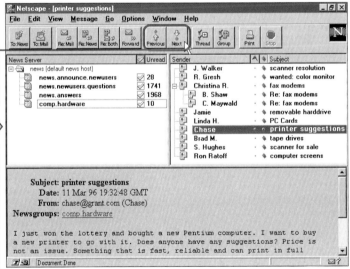

■ Articles you have not read display a diamond (◆) and appear in **bold** type.

2 To select an article you want to read, move the mouse ⤒ over the article and then press the left button.

■ This area displays the contents of the article.

Note: To view more of the contents, use the scroll bar. For more information, refer to page 23.

3 To quickly flip through unread articles in a newsgroup, move the mouse ⤒ over one of these options and then press the left button.

Displays previous unread article.

Displays next unread article.

Note: If you have read all the articles in the newsgroup, these options are not available.

You can reply to an article to answer a question, express an opinion or supply additional information.

Reply to an article only when you have something important to say. Replying "Me too" or "I agree" is not very informative.

REPLY TO AN ARTICLE

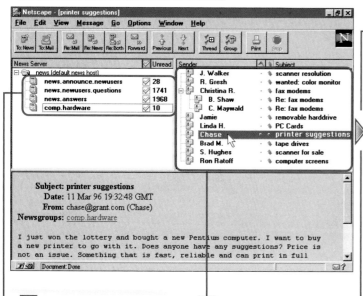

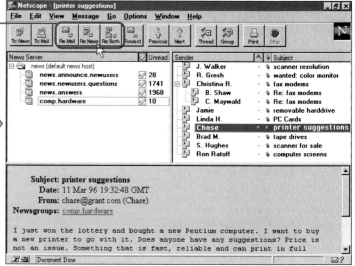

1 Move the mouse ⌖ over the newsgroup that contains the article you want to reply to and then press the left button.

2 Move the mouse ⌖ over the article and then press the left button.

3 Move the mouse ⌖ over a reply option and then press the left button.

 Replies to author - useful if your response would not be of interest to others in the newsgroup or you want to send a private response.

Replies to newsgroup.

Replies to author and newsgroup.

Tip

You can send your reply to the author of the article, the entire newsgroup or both the author and the newsgroup.

Newsgroup

Author

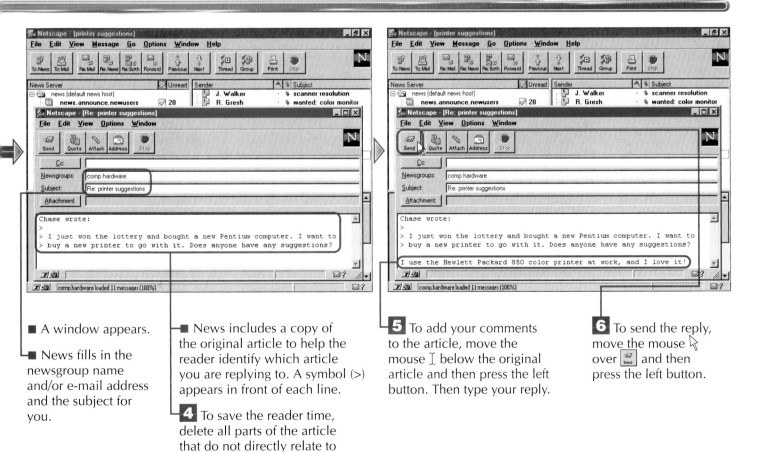

■ A window appears.

■ News fills in the newsgroup name and/or e-mail address and the subject for you.

■ News includes a copy of the original article to help the reader identify which article you are replying to. A symbol (>) appears in front of each line.

4 To save the reader time, delete all parts of the article that do not directly relate to your reply.

5 To add your comments to the article, move the mouse I below the original article and then press the left button. Then type your reply.

6 To send the reply, move the mouse over [Send] and then press the left button.

You can send a new article to a newsgroup to ask a question or express an opinion.

Thousands of people around the world will be able to read an article you post.

POST A NEW ARTICLE

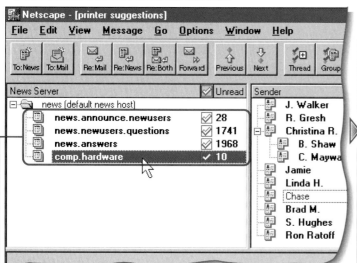

1 Move the mouse ⊹ over the newsgroup you want to post an article to and then press the left button.

*Note: If you want to practice posting an article, send an article to the **alt.test** newsgroup. Do not send practice articles to other newsgroups.*

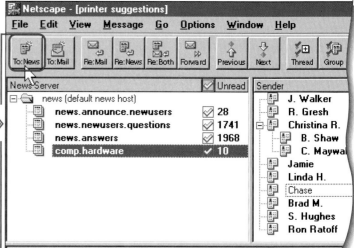

2 Move the mouse ⊹ over 📰 and then press the left button.

■ A window appears.

Tip

Read the articles in a newsgroup for a week before posting an article. This is called lurking. Lurking is a good way to learn how people in a newsgroup communicate and prevents you from posting information others have already read.

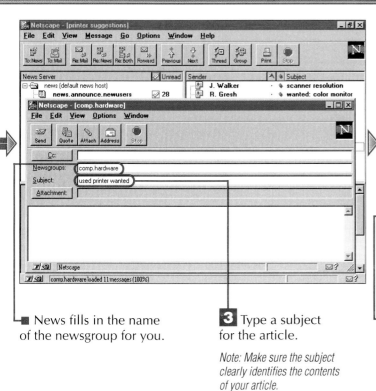

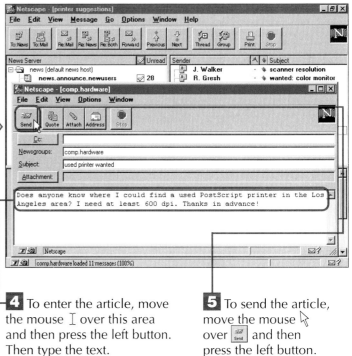

■ News fills in the name of the newsgroup for you.

3 Type a subject for the article.

Note: Make sure the subject clearly identifies the contents of your article.

4 To enter the article, move the mouse I over this area and then press the left button. Then type the text.

Note: Make sure the text you type is clear, concise and contains no spelling or grammar errors.

5 To send the article, move the mouse ↖ over 📧 and then press the left button.

After reading
an article, you can add
comments and then send
the article to a friend
or colleague.

FORWARD AN ARTICLE

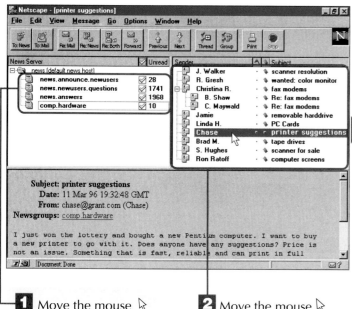

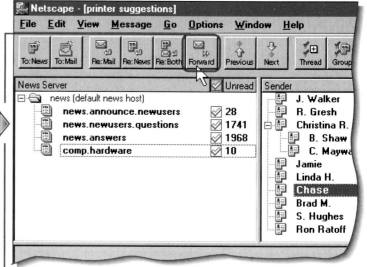

1 Move the mouse ⬚ over the newsgroup that contains the article you want to forward and then press the left button.

2 Move the mouse ⬚ over the article and then press the left button.

3 Move the mouse ⬚ over ⬚ and then press the left button.

■ A window appears.

Tip

When your friend or colleague receives an article you have forwarded, your comments and the newsgroup article appear in separate sections in the message.

Subject: [Fwd: printer suggestions]
Date: Mon, 08 Apr 1996 09:56:07 -0400
From: Mary Vickers <editorc@maran.com>
Organization: maranGraphics
To: msmith@sales.maran.com

Mike, I know you're interested in printers. Do you have any suggestions?

Subject: printer suggestions
Date: Mon, 11 Mar 1996 19:32:48 GMT
From: chase@grant.com
Newsgroups: comp.hardware

I just won the lottery and bought a new Pentium computer. I want to buy a new printer to go with it. Does anyone have any suggestions? Price is not an issue. Something that is fast, reliable and can print in full color. Thanks in advance.

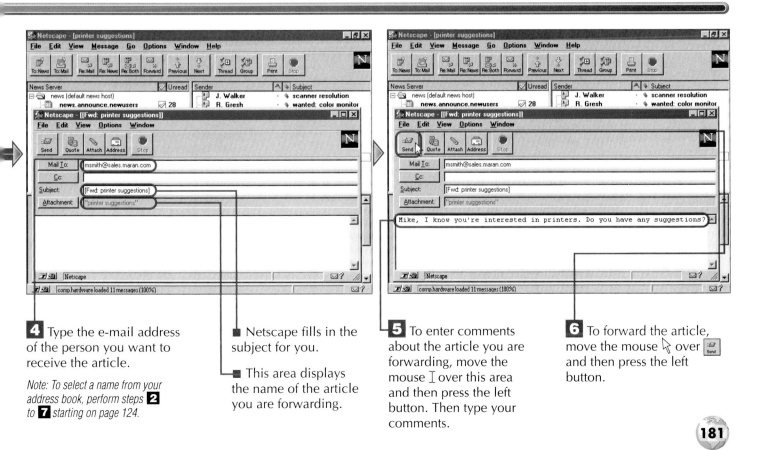

4 Type the e-mail address of the person you want to receive the article.

*Note: To select a name from your address book, perform steps **2** to **7** starting on page 124.*

■ Netscape fills in the subject for you.

■ This area displays the name of the article you are forwarding.

5 To enter comments about the article you are forwarding, move the mouse I over this area and then press the left button. Then type your comments.

6 To forward the article, move the mouse ⬚ over and then press the left button.

You can produce a paper copy of an article displayed on your screen.

PRINT AN ARTICLE

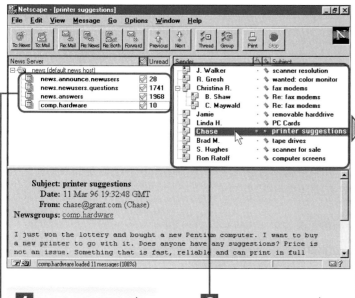

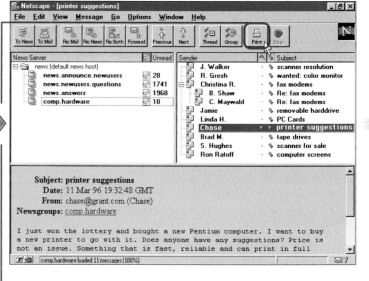

1 Move the mouse ↖ over the newsgroup that contains the article you want to print and then press the left button.

2 Move the mouse ↖ over the article and then press the left button.

3 Move the mouse ↖ over ⎙ and then press the left button.

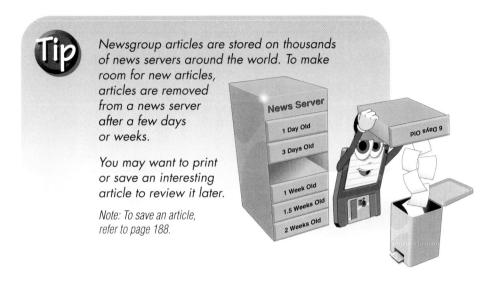

Tip Newsgroup articles are stored on thousands of news servers around the world. To make room for new articles, articles are removed from a news server after a few days or weeks.

You may want to print or save an interesting article to review it later.

Note: To save an article, refer to page 188.

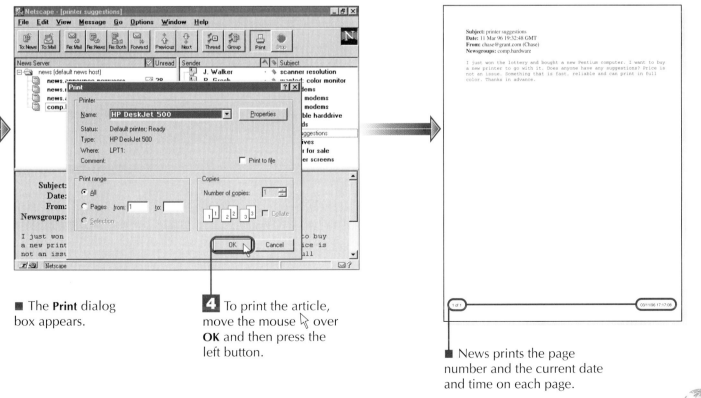

■ The **Print** dialog box appears.

4 To print the article, move the mouse ⤢ over **OK** and then press the left button.

■ News prints the page number and the current date and time on each page.

You can sort articles to help you more easily find articles of interest.

SORT ARTICLES

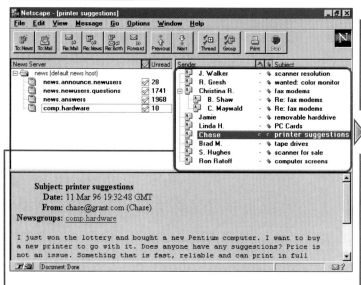

- News automatically sorts articles by date.

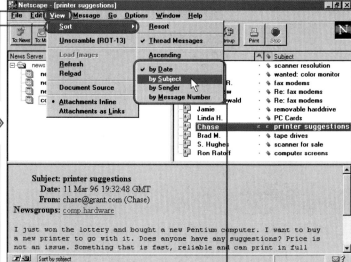

1 To change the way News sorts articles, move the mouse over **View** and then press the left button.

2 Move the mouse over **Sort**.

3 Move the mouse over the way you want to sort the articles and then press the left button.

Note: For more information, refer to the top of page 185.

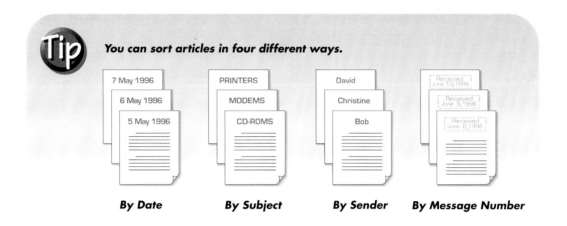

You can sort articles in four different ways.

7 May 1996	PRINTERS	David	Received June 10, 1996
6 May 1996	MODEMS	Christine	Received June 9, 1996
5 May 1996	CD-ROMS	Bob	Received June 8, 1996

By Date   ***By Subject***   ***By Sender***   ***By Message Number***

QUICKLY SORT ARTICLES

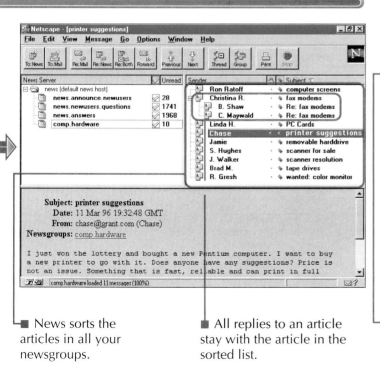

■ News sorts the articles in all your newsgroups.

■ All replies to an article stay with the article in the sorted list.

1 To quickly sort articles, move the mouse ▷ over the heading you want to sort by and then press the left button.

Note: If you cannot see the heading you want to sort by, you can enlarge the viewing area. To do so, refer to page 115.

■ News sorts the articles in all your newsgroups.

You can quickly locate an article of interest by searching the subject of each article in a newsgroup. This is useful when a newsgroup contains a lot of articles.

FIND AN ARTICLE

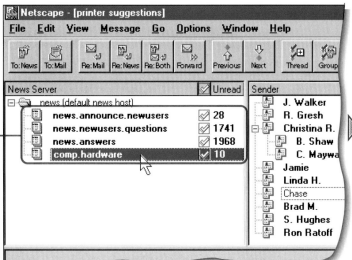

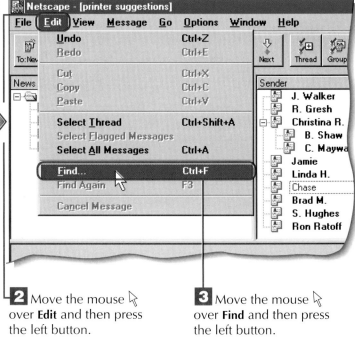

1 Move the mouse ⬚ over the newsgroup that contains the article you want to find and then press the left button.

2 Move the mouse ⬚ over **Edit** and then press the left button.

3 Move the mouse ⬚ over **Find** and then press the left button.

■ The **Find** dialog box appears.

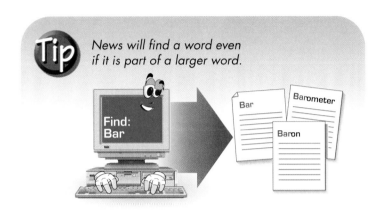

Tip

News will find a word even if it is part of a larger word.

Find: Bar

Bar

Barometer

Baron

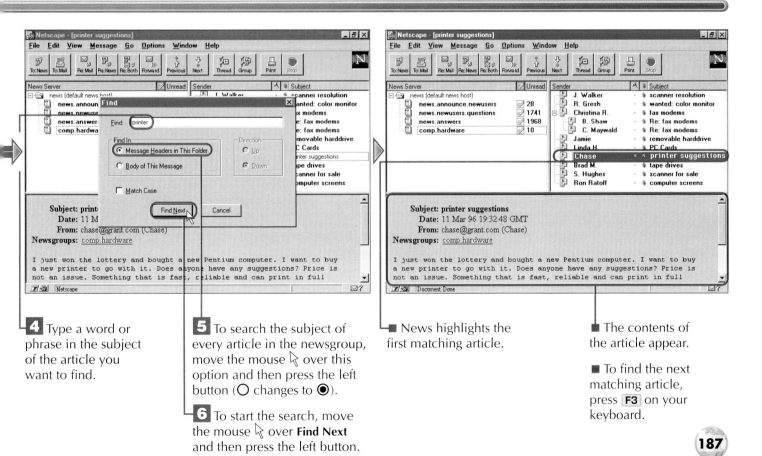

4 Type a word or phrase in the subject of the article you want to find.

5 To search the subject of every article in the newsgroup, move the mouse ⌖ over this option and then press the left button (○ changes to ◉).

6 To start the search, move the mouse ⌖ over **Find Next** and then press the left button.

■ News highlights the first matching article.

■ The contents of the article appear.

■ To find the next matching article, press **F3** on your keyboard.

You can save an article so you can view it when you are no longer connected to the Internet.

SAVE AN ARTICLE

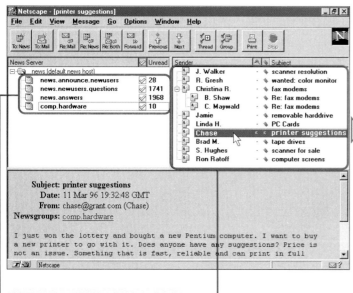

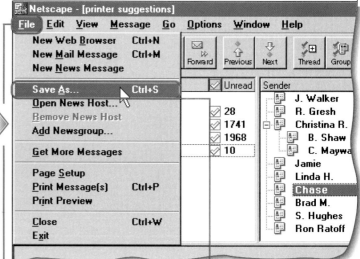

1 Move the mouse ⬚ over the newsgroup that contains the article you want to save and then press the left button.

2 Move the mouse ⬚ over the article and then press the left button.

3 Move the mouse ⬚ over **File** and then press the left button.

4 Move the mouse ⬚ over **Save As** and then press the left button.

■ The **Save As** dialog box appears.

You can easily open a saved article in Netscape.

1 To exit News, refer to page 165.

2 To open a saved article, perform steps **1** to **6** starting on page 46.

Note: You can also open a saved article in a word processing program, such as WordPad.

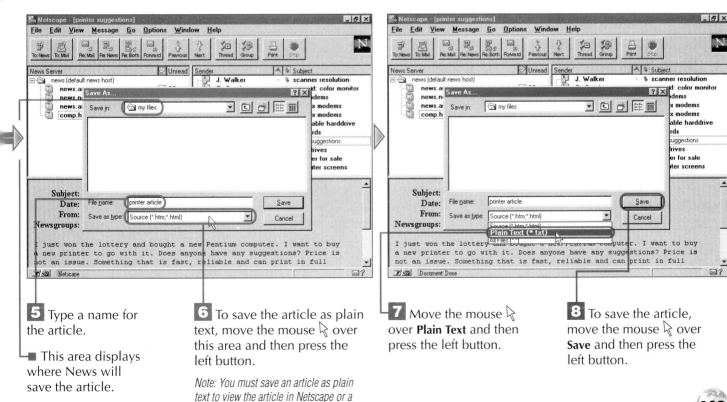

5 Type a name for the article.

■ This area displays where News will save the article.

6 To save the article as plain text, move the mouse ⬚ over this area and then press the left button.

Note: You must save an article as plain text to view the article in Netscape or a word processing program.

7 Move the mouse ⬚ over **Plain Text** and then press the left button.

8 To save the article, move the mouse ⬚ over **Save** and then press the left button.

189

CHANGE DISPLAY OF ARTICLES

You can specify which articles you want to display on your screen.

CHANGE DISPLAY OF ARTICLES

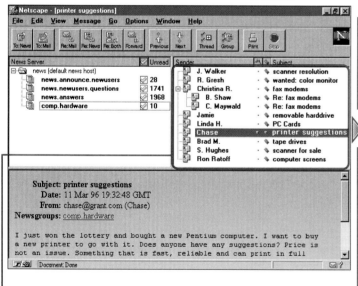

■ News automatically displays only the articles you have not read.

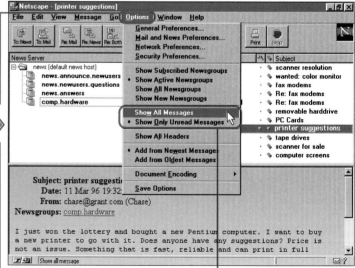

1 To change which articles appear on your screen, move the mouse ⌖ over **Options** and then press the left button.

2 Move the mouse ⌖ over the articles you want to display and then press the left button.

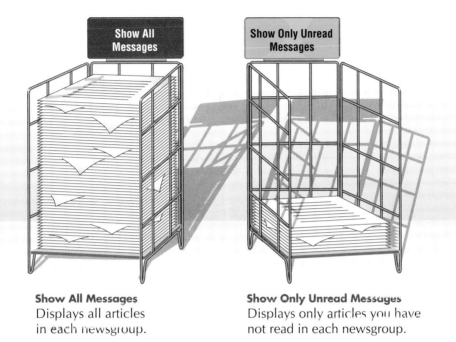

Show All Messages
Displays all articles
in each newsgroup.

Show Only Unread Messages
Displays only articles you have
not read in each newsgroup.

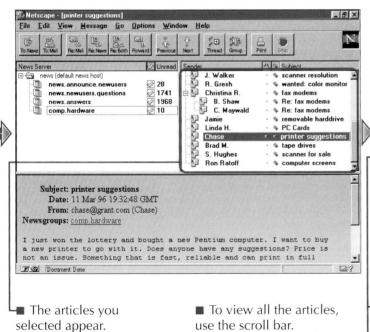

■ The articles you
selected appear.

■ To view all the articles,
use the scroll bar.

*Note: For more information,
refer to page 23.*

■ Articles you have not
read display a diamond (◆)
and appear in **bold** type.

■ Articles you have read
appear in plain type.

*Note: Articles are removed from a
news server after a few days or
weeks. If you cannot find an article
you have previously read, the
article may no longer exist on the
news server.*

GET MORE ARTICLES

Netscape only retrieves 100 articles from a newsgroup at once. If there are other articles available, you can easily display them.

GET MORE ARTICLES

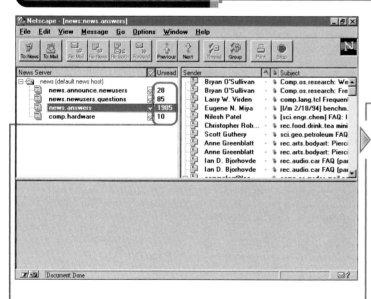

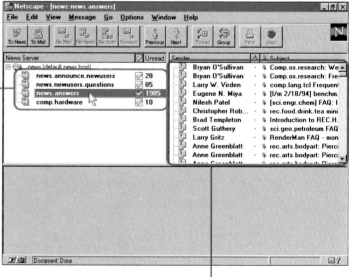

■ This area displays the number of articles you have not read in each newsgroup. If the number is over 100, you can have Netscape retrieve more articles so you can view them.

1 To get more articles, move the mouse ▷ over the newsgroup and then press the left button.

■ This area displays more articles for you to read.

MARK ARTICLES AS READ

When you finish reading all the articles of interest in a newsgroup, you can make all the articles appear as if you have read them.

The next time you view the articles in the newsgroup, only new articles will appear in **bold** text.

MARK ARTICLES AS READ

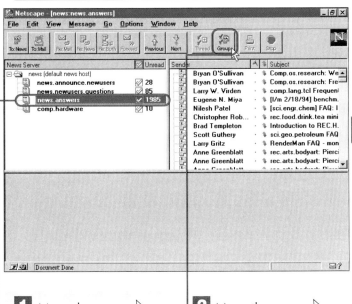

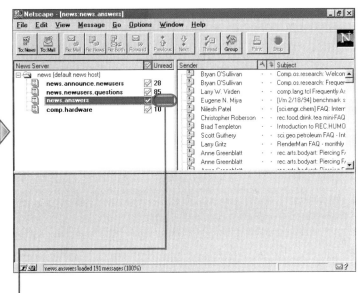

1 Move the mouse ⌖ over the newsgroup that contains the articles you want to mark as read and then press the left button.

2 Move the mouse ⌖ over 🔲 and then press the left button.

■ News clears the number of articles you have not read in the newsgroup.

CHAPTER 12

80 COOL WEB SITES

 Arts

 Business

 Government

 Health

 News

 Search Tools

 Sports

 Travel

 Weird

 What's Cool

Dancing on a Line

You will find information on performances, reviews and links to other sites.

URL *http://www.cipsinc.com/dance/doal.html*

Internet Movie Database

This enormous database provides information on movies from around the world.

URL *http://us.imdb.com*

Internet Underground Music Archive

A cool place to hear independent artists and bands.

URL *http://www.iuma.com*

Mr. Showbiz

Mr. Showbiz provides page after page of entertainment information and was nominated for "Cool Site of the Year."

URL *http://web3.starwave.com/showbiz*

Streetsound

A site dedicated to dance music and DJs.

URL *http://www.streetsound.com/zone*

TVNet

A great site for couch potatoes.

URL *http://www.tvnet.com*

Ultimate Band List

Looking for the home page for The Beatles or Madonna? Try here.

URL *http://american.recordings.com/wwwofmusic/ubl/ubl.shtml*

WebMuseum

View the works of famous artists like Monet, Rembrandt and Renoir.

URL *http://www.emf.net/louvre*

BUSINESS

American Express

Don't surf the Internet without it.

URL *http://www.americanexpress.com*

Coin Universe

A guide to pocket change.

URL *http://www.coin-universe.com/index.html*

Internet Shopping Network

A great site with discounts and weekly specials on computers, electronics and office products.

URL *http://www.internet.net*

Money Magazine

A great source of financial information.

URL *http://www.pathfinder.com/money*

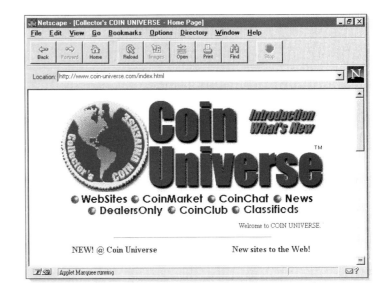

PC Quote

A great place to get delayed stock quotes.

URL *http://www.pcquote.com*

Ragú

This is a top-notch site with recipes, contests and guides to speaking Italian.

URL *http://www.eat.com*

VISA

VISA is making leaps and bounds in Internet technology and aims to create more secure online commerce in years to come.

URL *http://www.visa.com*

World Bank

Find out about the bank that lends developing countries money.

URL *http://www.worldbank.org*

GOVERNMENT

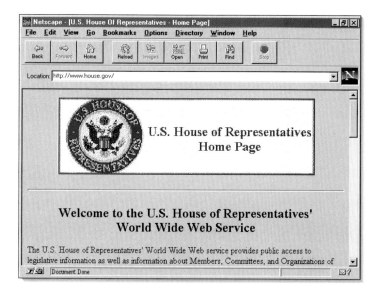

Welcome to the U.S. House of Representatives' World Wide Web Service

The U.S. House of Representatives' World Wide Web service provides public access to legislative information as well as information about Members, Committees, and Organizations of

Army

This site provides a great deal of information on the U.S. Army and links to other related sites.

URL http://www.army.mil

Canadiana

Everything you ever wanted to know about Canada.

URL http://www.cs.cmu.edu/Web/Unofficial/Canadiana/README.html

Department of Justice

They fight to protect your rights. This site has links to many agencies, including the FBI.

URL http://www.usdoj.gov

ElectionLine

Keep up-to-date on the current election news.

URL http://www.electionline.com

House of Representatives

Have you hugged your representative today?

URL http://www.house.gov

Thomas Library

This immense site has copies of bills and legislative information.

URL http://thomas.loc.gov

United Nations

This worldly organization has just celebrated its 50th anniversary by expanding its already extensive site.

URL http://www.un.org

Whitehouse

See the First Family or take a tour of the White House.

URL http://www.whitehouse.gov

HEALTH

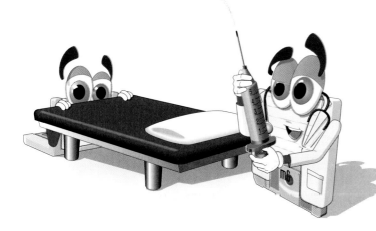

National Library of Medicine

Access medical and scientific research from this large collection.

URL *http://www.nlm.nih.gov/publications/publications.html*

Online AA Resources

Alcoholics Anonymous online information.

URL *http://matrix.casti.com:80/aa*

Veggies Unite!

An online guide to vegetarianism.

URL *http://www.honors.indiana.edu/~veggie/recipes.cgi*

World Health Organization

Find out all about the World Health Organization at this site.

URL *http://www.who.ch*

AIDS Memorial Quilt

Find out all about the quilt dedicated to those who have lost their lives to AIDS.

URL *http://www.aidsquilt.org*

American Medical Association

Medical journals and other information for doctors, scientists and students.

URL *http://www.ama-assn.org*

Centers for Disease Control and Prevention

Learn how to prevent and control many diseases, injuries and disabilities.

URL *http://www.cdc.gov*

Mental Health Info Link

Online psychological resources for professionals and the general public.

URL *http://www.onlinepsych.com/treat/mh.htm*

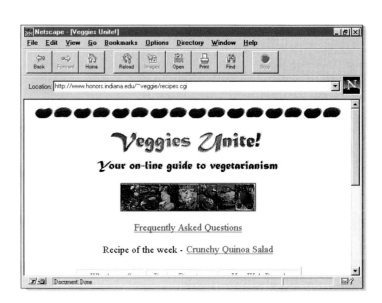

clnet Central

The online site of clnet, the weekly computer show on cable.

URL *http://www.cnet.com*

CNN Interactive

CNN is one of the world's most popular all-news television networks. You can find the latest news, weather reports, sports and much more at this site.

URL *http://www.cnn.com*

Electric Library

This site claims to be the Internet's largest digital collection of newspapers and magazines.

URL *http://www.elibrary.com*

New York Times

One of the most recognized newspapers in North America.

URL *http://www.nytimes.com*

Pathfinder

Time Warner has put most of its magazines online here, including Time, People and Sports Illustrated.

URL *http://www.pathfinder.com*

U.S. News and World Report

News you can use.

URL *http://www.usnews.com*

USA Today

The newspaper famous for its surveys and charts has a large portion of its content online.

URL *http://www.usatoday.com*

Virtual Newspaper

Links to newspapers in the U.S. and around the world.

URL *http://www.refdesk.com/paper.html*

SEARCH TOOLS

Alta Vista

The best place to search for obscure topics.

URL *http://altavista.digital.com*

Excite!

Excite uses new technology to search for general concepts instead of the usual keyword search used by other sites.

URL *http://www.excite.com*

Infoseek

Infoseek continues to win awards for its fantastic searching capabilities.

URL *http://www.infoseek.com*

Lycos

Lycos maintains the A2Z Internet directory of some of the best sites on the Web.

URL *http://www.lycos.com*

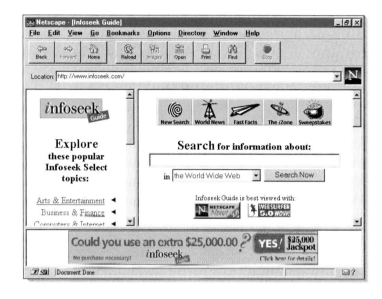

Open Text Index

This cutting-edge search tool helps you find information on the Web.

URL *http://www.opentext.com:8080*

WebCrawler

America Online funds this speedy search tool.

URL *http://www.webcrawler.com*

WhoWhere?

Finally, a site that lets you search for e-mail addresses.

URL *http://www.whowhere.com*

Yahoo

Yet Another Hierarchical Officious Oracle. Basically, it's a good place to browse through categories or search for a specific site.

URL *http://www.yahoo.com*

Baseball Links

Everything you ever wanted to know about America's favorite pastime.

URL *http://www.pc-professor.com/baseball/homepage.html*

ESPNET SportsZone

This site provides all a sports fan could want: scores, pictures, schedules and more.

URL *http://espnet.sportszone.com*

National Basketball Association

Find information on your favorite NBA teams and players.

URL *http://www.nba.com*

National Hockey League

They shoot, they score.

URL *http://www.nhl.com*

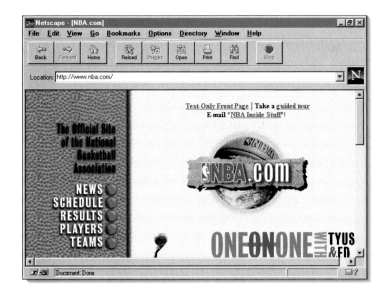

Olympics

A great site offering information on every aspect of the 1996 Olympic Games.

URL *http://www.atlanta.olympic.org*

Sports Network

Live score updates and articles on teams and players in many different sports.

URL *http://www.sportsnetwork.com*

Team NFL

The official home of the National Football League.

URL *http://nflhome.com*

TSN

A Canadian view of sports around the world.

URL *http://www.tsn.ca*

TRAVEL

American Airlines

Flight information and pricing details are available at this eye-catching site.

URL *http://www.amrcorp.com/aa_home/aa_home.htm*

Condé Nast Traveler

Find travel information on destinations around the world.

URL *http://www.cntraveler.com*

Delta Airlines

Delta has flight information and an online contest to win free tickets.

URL *http://www.delta-air.com/index.html*

Internet Travel Network

Book your entire trip from the comfort of your own computer.

URL *http://www.itn.net/cgi/get?itn/index*

Royal Caribbean Cruise Lines

This site features Cruise-O-Matic, an interactive destination finder.

URL *http://www.royalcaribbean.com*

Travel Channel

This site tells you which vacation spots are hot and which are not.

URL *http://www.travelchannel.com*

United Airlines

Find flight information, frequent flyer promotions and travel tips at this site.

URL *http://www.ual.com*

Web Travel Review

First-hand accounts from people who have traveled to countries around the world.

URL *http://webtravel.org/webtravel*

Centre for the Easily Amused

The ultimate guide to wasting time.

URL *http://www2.islandnet.com/~cwalker*

Cyrano Server

This site will write a love letter based on information you provide.

URL *http://www.nando.net/toys/cyrano.html*

Jingle Cats

Cats meow and hiss their way through Christmas classics online.

URL *http://jinglecats.com*

Kingdom of Talossa

A 13-year-old boy declared his bedroom a sovereign state. Now he's king!

URL *http://www.execpc.com/~talossa*

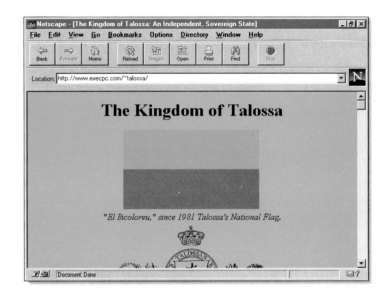

Netscape - [The Kingdom of Talossa: An Independent, Sovereign State]

File Edit View Go Bookmarks Options Directory Window Help

Back Forward Home Reload Images Open Print Find Stop

Location: http://www.execpc.com/~talossa/

The Kingdom of Talossa

"El Bicoloreu," since 1981 Talossa's National Flag.

Document: Done

Loser Living Upstairs

The tale of a mysterious loser who lives upstairs…don't ask.

URL *http://www.calpoly.edu/~ttokuuke/loser.html*

Really Big Button That Doesn't Do Anything

This useless page has received more visits than many distinguished online magazines.

URL *http://www.wam.umd.edu/~twoflowr/button.htm*

T.W.I.N.K.I.E.S. Project

Tests With Inorganic Noxious Kakes In Extreme Situations. Some people really do need to get a life.

URL *http://www.rice.edu/~gouge/twinkies.html*

Underground Net

Truly bizarre, it's never the same twice.

URL *http://bazaar.com*

WHAT'S COOL

Netscape What's Cool?

Having your site on this list will guarantee you thousands of visits a day.

URL *http://home.netscape.com/home/ whats-cool.html*

Project Cool

The man who created the Cool Site of the Day concept has gone on to create the fantastic Project Cool.

URL *http://www.projectcool.com*

Spider's Pick of the Day

The Spider puts up his daily pick of Internet sites.

URL *http://gagme.wwa.com/~boba/pick.html*

Too Cool Awards

The name really says it all.

URL *http://toocool.com*

Blazin' Bookmark

maranGraphics' weekly pick from the World Wide Web.

URL *http://www.maran.com/surf.html*

Cool Site of the Day

This popular site lists a new "cool" Web site every day of the year.

URL *http://cool.infi.net*

Dynamite Site of the Nite

A great place to find out what's new and hot on the Internet.

URL *http://www.netzone.com/~tti/dsotn.html*

Mirsky's Worst of the Web

Tired of finding what's cool? Mirsky lists all the sad, pathetic and shameless sites your heart desires.

URL *http://mirsky.turnpike.net/wow/Worst.html*

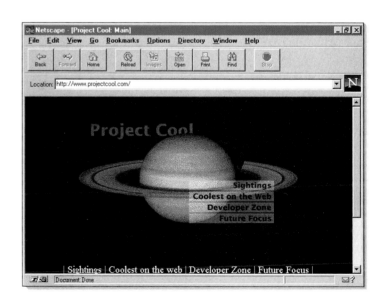

INDEX

INDEX

INDEX